Contents

...vertising Increase Smoking?

Economics, Free Speech and Advertising Bans

iea

...irs

First published in March 1999 by
The Institute of Economic Affairs
2 Lord North Street
Westminster
London SW1P 3LB

Occasional Paper 107

ISSN 0073-909X
ISBN 0-255 36423-7

Printed in Great Britain by
Hartington Fine Arts Limited, Lancing, West Sussex
Set in Times Roman 11 on 13 point

Foreword

ATTEMPTS TO ESTIMATE THE EFFECTS of advertising on sales go back at least to the 1950s and there is now a voluminous literature on the subject.

Econometric analysis of advertising elasticities has to confront some difficult issues. First, there is the usual problem in such analysis of controlling for all the variables other than advertising that appear to influence sales (so that the advertising effect can be isolated). But there are other problems which arise from the nature of advertising.

Advertisers try to persuade consumers to switch to their products but there are likely to be long and variable time lags in any sales response to advertising. Promotional expenditure now may continue to influence consumers for some considerable time into the future and past advertising may still be affecting their behaviour. Some authors have therefore argued that advertising is a means of building up a stock of goodwill – the existing stock is replenished by new advertising but depreciates as the effects of past advertising wear off. Such effects are difficult to model formally and many advertising models are simplistic and poorly specified, especially in not dealing well with time lags.

Another issue which arises when modelling the effects of advertising is whether it merely results in brand switching by consumers or whether there is likely to be some expansion in the total market for the products which are advertised. That question is very important in considering the likely effectiveness of restrictions on the advertising of products the consumption of which, for some reason, government would like to limit.

In Occasional Paper 107, Professor Hugh High steps carefully into this minefield, providing a valuable critical survey of models of the effects of tobacco advertising. After examining in some detail numerous models from both more developed and less developed countries, he concludes that '...there is no evidence that advertising of tobacco products leads to an increase in the total consumption of tobacco' (page 69) though it affects the market shares of individual brands.

Professor High also investigates the claim that tobacco advertising is particularly influential in inducing the young to begin smoking. Here again he finds no evidence that would support some of the drastic actions often advocated – such as the advertising bans proposed in a number of developed countries.

He sees restrictions on tobacco advertising from a liberal viewpoint as constraints on individual freedom to choose and freedom of information.

> 'Only those with a disdain for the rights of individuals and who wish to substitute decision-making by the "Nanny, or Orwellian, State" for decisions by free and independent individuals would support such restrictions.' (p. 117)

The 'burden of persuasion is especially heavy', he argues, when the state proposes restricting freedom of speech and of the press.

All IEA publications present the views of their authors, not those of the Institute (which has no corporate view), its Trustees, Advisers or Directors. Professor High's challenging paper is published to stimulate discussion of the controversial issues he raises.

March 1999

COLIN ROBINSON
Editorial Director, Institute of Economic Affairs
Professor of Economics, University of Surrey

The Author

HUGH HIGH RECEIVED his AB degree from Texas Christian University, Forth Worth, Texas, USA; his MA and PhD in economics from Duke University, Durham, North Carolina, and his JD (Juris Doctor) from Wake Forest University, Winston-Salem, North Carolina, USA. He is a member of the bar of the State of North Carolina.

He practised law for a short while, and has taught Economics, Finance and Law at various universities in America, New Zealand and South Africa. These include Wake Forest University, Massey University and the University of the Witwatersrand.

Among his publications are: 'Determination of Damages Awarded Under Exchange Rate Fluctuations', 'New Zealand's Economic and Financial Revolution', 'W.H. Hutt's Model of Racial Discrimination', 'The Theory and Practice of Labour Relations in South Africa', and 'The Economic Case for Insider Trading'.

He presently teaches Economics, Finance and Law at the University of Cape Town. His chief intellectual interests have gravitated to Law and Economics and Public Choice.

He is a member of the National Council of the Free Market Foundation of South Africa.

Acknowledgements

I SHOULD LIKE TO THANK SEVERAL PEOPLE WHO HAVE CONTRIBUTED to this undertaking and without whom it would be much inferior. First, my wife, M. Jane Hobson High, has endured my endless discussion of the topic, and my often emphatic outbursts at what I consider to be shoddy research work by a number of those working in this area. Patiently, she has realised that my interest sprang from a firm commitment to the belief that free speech, broadly conceived, requires defence against (particularly) those whom Hayek called 'intellectuals' and 'planners'. She recognised it is a commitment which I hold dear and which has continued to motivate me in this all too long, and often tiresome, undertaking.

Secondly, I owe a real debt of gratitude to those who allege they know best what is good for the rest of us – who know what we should read, see and hear – and who are determined they will use the might of government to ensure that we read, see and hear only that which, in their wisdom, they have determined is in our best interest. Without their arrogance and disregard for the importance of the fundamental civil liberties, and the right of the great mass of us to make choices for ourselves, I would not have been able to sustain my zeal for the completion of this work.

Were it not for the contributions (in no particular order, other than alphabetic) of Anonymous Readers, Roger Bate, Editors at the IEA, Lisa Mac Lellan, Julian Morris, and Colin Robinson, this work might still be languishing on disk, or in my files. Needless to say, the usual caveats apply.

1. Introduction

SOON AFTER THE 1997 ELECTION TONY BLAIR PROMISED early legislation to ban tobacco advertising. At much the same time, the American government proposed an agreement with the tobacco industry and anti-smoking advocates which would virtually eliminate tobacco advertising, which was deemed to 'entice' individuals, especially the young, to smoke.

Such proposals follow legislation in a number of countries to discourage or curb smoking. Restrictions on commercial 'speech' are typically justified on the grounds that the State has a duty, under its 'police powers', to promote the health of the citizenry which is adversely affected by smoking.

This paper examines the general legality and legal tests on restrictions on advertising in Anglo-American legal jurisdictions before reviewing the evidence on the effectiveness of commercial advertising in inducing people, the young in particular, to begin smoking. Clearly, if advertising does not induce people to begin smoking, restrictions cannot be justified. We are not concerned with the health issues,[1] but only with the presumed nexus between smoking and advertising.

---

1 This aspect has been most recently examined in *Murder a Cigarette,* London: Duckworth, 1998.

2. *The Legality of Restrictions on Advertising*

VIRTUALLY ALL MODERN SOCIETIES include 'free speech' as one of the fundamental rights enjoyed by their citizens. In practice, this means that when politicians attempt to restrict the right of 'free speech', the judiciary is empowered to scrutinise the proposed restrictions and prohibit the state from interfering with the right of citizens to communicate with their fellows. To employ the language of American jurisprudence, 'free speech' is so important in modern democratic societies that it is deemed a 'suspect category'; that is, a right held so vital to the preservation of liberty that any proposed restriction is 'suspected' of being a violation of fundamental and/or constitutional rights and guarantees, such that the state has a special burden of demonstrating any proposed restrictions are crucial and vital – and not merely convenient – for the performance and execution of otherwise legitimate state functions if proposed restrictions are upheld as valid. This is as true in countries, like the UK, which have a 'Westminster', or 'parliamentary supremacy' system of government and no expressly written constitution, as with countries like the USA which have written constitutions and a more clearly delineated separation of legislative, executive, and judicial powers. The economic, as distinct from the political or philosophical, rationale for encouraging 'free speech', and particularly 'commercial free speech', is that it helps move the economy in the direction of increasing competition. One of the textbook requirements of a perfectly competitive economy is 'perfect information'; while economists recognise that this condition is never fully satisfied, they would argue that wide dissemination of information about goods and services will make markets increasingly efficient.

In no country is the right of 'free speech' absolute. Invariably, governmental restrictions on defamatory, obscene or seditious speech, for example, have been upheld. Similarly, most nations permit governments to restrict 'speech' or 'print' when it serves to protect a 'greater' right, such as the right of a criminal defendant to a fair trial. The relevant question for our purposes is the specific conditions under which the state is permitted to curtail the right of free speech.

The Legal Status of 'Free Speech' in Commercial Advertising

While both statutory and case law vary from jurisdiction to jurisdiction among 'Anglo-American' countries, the general principles governing the legal right of the state to restrict commercial advertising are, not surprisingly, similar, reflecting a general recognition of the importance of free speech. We shall briefly examine the general legal principles which govern the right and ability of the state to restrict advertising, without pretending that each of the jurisdictions adheres precisely to the general rules.

The general Anglo-American approach is illustrated by the legal rules laid down by the Canadian Supreme Court in the landmark Oakes case of 1986,[1] which were later employed in a much-heralded case on tobacco advertising (RJR-MacDonald, 1991[2]). The Oakes test lays down hurdles which the state must overcome before abridging the rights Canadian citizens enjoy under the Charter of Rights and Freedoms, which is Canada's equivalent of the American 'Bill of Rights'. Specifically, under the Oakes test, the government must satisfy two basic criteria.

First, the government must establish that the objective of its proposed limitation of the citizen's right is of 'sufficient importance to warrant over-riding a constitutionally protected right or freedom'. Objectives 'which are trivial or discordant with the principles integral to a free and democratic society...'[3] will result in judicial disapproval of the government's proposed limitations of rights.

Second, even if the court agrees that the regulation of 'free speech' does advance a sufficiently significant objective, the government must further show that 'the means chosen are

---

1 *Regina v. Oakes* [1986], 26 D. L. R. (4th) 200, 24 C.C.C. (3d) 321, 1 S.C. R. 103.

2 *RJR-MacDonald, Inc. v. Attorney General of Canada*, 82 D.L.R. 4th 449 [1991] and 102 D.L.R. 4th [1993].

3 *Oakes*, as per Dickson C. J. C., at 225–228 citing *R. v. Big M. Drug Mart Ltd.* [1985] 18 D. L. R. (4th) 321, 18 C.C. C. (3d) 385, 1 S.C.R. 295, 85 A.R. 161, 58 N.R. 81.

reasonable and demonstrably justified'. In making this determination, the Canadian courts follow a 'proportionality test' specified by the Supreme Court as having three parts. *First*, the government must demonstrate that the measures it employs are carefully designed to achieve its objective. *Second*, it must demonstrate that the means employed 'impair as little as possible the right or freedom in question'. *Finally*, there must be 'proportionality' between the means the government proposes to restrict the fundamental right of free speech, and the effects of the restrictive legislation. In other words, government must demonstrate that the restrictions on liberty are absolutely no greater than necessary to attain the otherwise permissible governmental objective, and can be no more than 'proportional' to the benefits likely to be forthcoming from the proposed restriction.

Thus, at every step, the burden is on the state to demonstrate to the satisfaction of the judiciary that the proposed restriction is necessary to attain a permissible governmental objective, restricts individual freedom to the minimum extent, and is 'proportional' to the expected benefits from the restriction on freedom.

The importance of 'perfect knowledge' was echoed by the Canadian Supreme Court in its recognition that if producers are obstructed in providing information to consumers, 'informed economic choices' would not be possible. The Canadian courts have noted that:

> 'commercial expression ... plays a significant role in enabling individuals to make informed economic choices, an important aspect of individual self-fulfilment and personal autonomy.'[4]

Accordingly, legislation which attempts to restrict the ability of individuals to make informed choices, such as excessive restrictions on commercial advertising, will generally not receive judicial sanction in Anglo-American jurisdictions.

In striking down the attempt by the Canadian government to restrict the right of tobacco companies to advertise, and of readers/listeners to read/listen to such advertising, Mr Justice

---

[4] *RJR* as per Chabot, Justice J.J. at 498–99 citing *Ford v Quebec (Attorney-General)* (988), 54 D.L. R. (4th) 577, [1988] 2 S.C.R. 712, 36 C.R. R. 1, 10 C.H.R.R. d/5559, 19 Q.A.C. 69, 90 N.R. 84.

Chabot of the Canadian Supreme Court said:

> 'The State seeks to control the thoughts, beliefs and behaviour of its citizens along the lines that it considers acceptable. This form of paternalism is unacceptable in a free and democratic society such as ours...'[5]

Crucial aspects of these judicial tests are the requirements that the governmental restrictions (a) are likely to achieve their proclaimed objective and (b) are the least restrictive means of so doing. It follows that when governments endeavour to restrict commercial advertising of tobacco products in the belief that such restrictions will lead to a decrease in consumption, the burden of proof is on them to demonstrate that consumption is likely to be decreased. If advertising does not serve to increase the total demand, then governments cannot meet this burden and the proposed legislation will not pass judicial scrutiny. It is to the evidence on the relationship between advertising and consumption that we now turn.

---

[5] *RJR v McDonald*, *op. cit.*, cited in John Luik, *Freedom of Expression*, St Catherines, Ontario: Gray Matters Press, 1991, p. 1.

3. *Preliminary Observations on Advertising*

THE CONVENTIONAL RATIONALE OF THE RIGHT OF GOVERNMENT to restrict tobacco advertising is protection of the health of the citizenry and particularly of younger members of society who are alleged to be both particularly deserving of protection and particularly susceptible to the lure of commercial tobacco advertising.

We do not here enter into the question of the health effects of smoking tobacco products, but if a government believes that consumption of tobacco products impairs the health of consumers, we might understand it considering outlawing all consumption. Yet governments have not done so for a number of reasons. The general history of prohibition of alcohol, and other products, clearly demonstrates that it does not so much curb consumption as raise their prices and usually gives rise to various criminal acts related to sale of the prohibited product. The ill-fated history of American prohibition is well known to even the most ignorant parliamentarian.

Since in most Western countries, tobacco continues to be consumed by around a third of all adults who are also voters, outright prohibition would surely be met with the stiffest opposition. Furthermore, taxation of tobacco is an important source of government revenue. Consequently, instead of an outright ban on the sale and consumption of tobacco products, governments have responded with lesser political pressures, suggesting that governments do not find the health threat so dire as to justify prohibition.

Interestingly, belief that tobacco advertising increases smoking is quite new. Fewer than 25 years ago, in 1975, Karl Warnberg of Sweden, addressing the Third World Conference on Smoking and Health, said :

> 'No empirical research has been able to show that aggregate brand advertising leads to greater total tobacco consumption. Nor has anything been found to suggest that advertising entices non-smokers, young people in particular, into becoming smokers. It follows,

therefore, that there can be no evidence that a ban on advertising would result in reduced tobacco consumption and fewer new smokers.'[1]

At this same conference Professor James L. Hamilton, a professor of Marketing at Wayne State University in Ohio, noted that cigarette advertising by tobacco companies was invariably employed as a 'competitive weapon' (against rival brands) and 'has not been used as a means for expanding the market'. [2]

Similarly, in 1982, the Task Force on Smoking of the Province of Ontario, Canada, concluded that 'no persuasive empirical evidence exists' to support the argument that advertising is a significant determinant of smoking.[3] This was followed in 1983 by the statement of Michael Pertschuk, former Chairman of the US Federal Trade Commission – who now assists the anti-smoking Advocacy Institute – that 'no one really pretends that advertising is a ... major determinant of smoking in this country'.[4] In 1985, Elizabeth Whelan of the American Council on Health doubted that an advertising ban would reduce cigarette consumption. [5]

Indeed, as recently as 1989 the US Surgeon General, C. Everett Koop, acknowledged that cigarette advertising and promotion had not been shown to increase tobacco consumption:

> 'There is no scientifically rigorous study available to the public that provides a definitive answer to the basic question of whether advertising and promotion increase the level of tobacco consumption.'[6]

---

[1] Karl Warnberg, 'Ban on Advertising – What Then?', *II Proceedings of the 3rd World Conference on Smoking and Health*, New York: *The World Conference on Smoking and Health*, 1975, p. 854.

[2] J. L. Hamilton, 'The Effects of Cigarette Advertising Bans on Cigarette Consumption', *II Proceedings of the 3rd World Conference on Smoking and Health*, New York: *The World Conference on Smoking and Health*, 1975, pp. 830–31.

[3] Province of Ontario, *Task Force on Smoking. Smoking and Health in Ontario: A Need for Balance*, 1982, p. 104.

[4] Harvard University, 'Tobacco Issues', Cambridge, Mass.: Harvard University Institute of Politics, Cassette 1. Tr. 8 (27 April 1983).

[5] 'Second Thoughts on a Cigarette-Ad Ban', *Wall Street Journal*, 18 December 1985, p. 28, col. 6.

[6] US Dept. of Health and Human Services, *Reducing the Health Consequences of Smoking:*

Moreover, on smoking by young people, as early as 1969 data of the American Cancer Society presented to the US Congress demonstrated the power of example in shaping smoking behaviour: 'where parents or other frequently-seen adults smoke, youngsters are more likely to take up the habit. [Indeed] most influential of all seems to be friends.'[7]

These observations were, as we shall see below, correct in suggesting no relationship between tobacco consumption and advertising either among adults or younger persons. It is difficult to understand why, aside from propaganda, those concerned about smoking should divert resources and attention to the effects of advertising.

The belief that advertising might lead to increased consumption or induce non-smokers to begin smoking is, like the invention of 'passive smoking', largely a product of the last decade or so (Hatton and Harris, 1998, pp. 125-41).

The Nature of Advertising in 'Mature' Product Markets

Virtually all companies, including monopolies, advertise. Much of this advertising is not intended to increase the number of people who use the 'product category'. Rather, advertising is employed for a variety of reasons depending on whether the product is in a 'new product' category or a 'mature' one and on whether the product category is in competition with other categories.[8]

With new product categories such as cellular telephones, video-cassette recorders or personal computers, advertising aims to inform people about their general attributes and benefits, rather than to promote a particular *brand*. As consumer awareness of the product category expands, advertising faces a mature market.

A Report of the Surgeon General, 1989, p. 512.

[7] *Advertising of Tobacco Products: Hearings Before the Subcommittee on Health and the Environment of the House Committee on Energy and Commerce*, 99th Congress, 1st Sess., 683 (1986). [Statement of Prof. Scott Ward.]

[8] For a general discussion of the purposes of advertising, and particularly the concept of a 'product life cycle' and the role of promotion of mature product categories see, *inter alia*, C.R. Wasson, *Dynamic Competitive Strategy and Product Life Cycle*, 1978; R. Polli and V. Cook, 'Validity of the Product Life Cycle,' *J. Bus.*, October 1978; R.G. Hammermesh and S. B. Silk, 'How to Compete in Stagnant Industries', *Harvard Business Review*, September-October 1979.

Examples of mature markets include petrol, toothpaste, soap, laundry detergent, telephones, and television sets. There is a large literature which demonstrates that in such mature markets advertising is not significantly related to aggregate product demand but aims to raise demand for the advertised brand.[9] This fact was even acknowledged, as recently as 1994, by the US Institute of Medicine.[10]

Nonetheless, it has been argued by some, including the American Food and Drug Administration (FDA), that cigarettes are not a mature market because the tobacco industry must continue to advertise so as to 'lure' young people into the market. This reflects a total failure to understand what is meant by a mature product.

The simple fact is that every mature market – whether automobiles, houses, television sets, cigarettes, washing machines, and so on – has first-time buyers who have never previously purchased the product. Manufacturers of cigarettes are no more dependent on new buyers than are other manufacturers of mature products. It is entirely rational for manufacturers of goods in mature markets to advertise in order to increase or maintain their existing market share. In the UK, total annual sales of cigarettes are over £12 billion so that gaining an additional 1 per cent share means gaining sales of well over £100 million. [11]

The importance of maintaining market share is especially acute in the British tobacco industry which is faced by evidence that more than 1 in 3 smokers switch brands every year. Advertising, then, is a highly effective way to ensure that keen competition exists in the tobacco market-place which bans and restrictions on

---

[9] A review of some of this literature is to be found in D.A. Aaker and J.M. Carment, 'Are You Over Advertising?: A Review of Advertising-Sales Studies', *J. Advertising Research*, Vol. 22 (4) (August–September 1982), as well as J. Yasin, 'The Effects of Advertising on Fast Moving Consumer Markets', *Int'l. J. of Advertising*, Vol. 14, 1995, pp. 133–47. The latter is a study of 42 consumer goods markets, including tobacco, which concluded that 'there is no consistent correlation between advertising levels and total market growth'. These studies validate the theoretical and empirical findings of L. G. Telser, 'Advertising and Cigarettes', *J. Pol. Economy*, Vol. 70, 1962. In a landmark of 'consumption-demand' literature, Telser established that advertising in 'mature markets' shifted demand amongst firms rather than altering total market demand.

[10] Institute of Medicine, *Growing Up Tobacco Free*, Washington: US G. P. O., 1994, p. 105.

[11] See J. Yasir, 'The Effects of Advertising on Fast-Moving Consumer Goods Markets', 14 *Int'l. J. of Advertising*, 1995, pp. 145–46.

advertising can only stifle, thereby entrenching established firms.

In conclusion, it should be emphasised that were advertising of tobacco products to be banned, it would be more difficult for consumers to acquire knowledge of new products, including cigarettes with lower tar and nicotine and so-called 'smokeless' cigarettes. It would therefore inhibit the development of such products, as well as making it more difficult for new entrants with 'specialised' products to enter the market.

4. *Review of Major International Studies of the Advertising-Consumption Relationship*

THERE IS A VOLUMINOUS LITERATURE on the relationship between advertising and tobacco consumption. Given this literature and its widely varying quality – a fact ignored by the UK 'Smee Report' – we have grouped the studies into three: (a) cross-sectional, or international, studies, which are examined in this section; (b) time-series national studies, which are discussed in Section 5; and (c) studies concentrating on the relationship between advertising and consumption among the young, which are the subject of Section 6.

The 1989 Report of the New Zealand Toxic Substances Board – The 'TSB' Study

Perhaps the most widely known study of the relationship between advertising and tobacco consumption is the 1989 Report of the New Zealand Toxic Substances Board, entitled *Health or Tobacco: An End to Tobacco Advertising and Promotion.*[1] This 139-page report, which has become known in the literature as the TSB Report, concluded on the basis of tobacco consumption and price data from most OECD countries for the period 1970-86, that 'total elimination of tobacco advertising can be expected to permanently lower cigarette consumption by 7 percent below what it would have been in the absence of such a ban'. If correct, such a finding would represent a strong *a priori* case for those who would ban tobacco advertising. However, the Attorney-General of Canada came to regret employing the TSB Report as a principal weapon in the abortive defence of Canada's legislative ban on tobacco advertising.

The simple fact is that the TSB report was shown to be so flawed in its data and methodology that Mr Justice Jean-Jude Chabot of the Canadian Superior Court was led in 1991 to say:

---

[1] New Zealand Dept. of Health, Toxic Substances Board, *Health or Tobacco: an End to Tobacco Advertising and Promotion*, Wellington, N.Z., 1989.

'With respect to the T.S.B. Report, the Court can only note that it contains serious methodological errors and a lack of scientific rigor which renders it for all intents and purposes devoid of any probative value. It is a report with an obvious point of view and its conclusions reflect that point of view. In this regard, the Court...concludes that the T.S.B. Report, as an extrinsic document, is of no probative value.'[2]

It is nevertheless worth reviewing in some detail not only because it has received wide attention, especially in the popular press, but because it has spawned much of the current literature on the alleged relationship between advertising and tobacco consumption. It also serves as an important case study of the way legislatures uncritically and hastily adopt policy recommendations of allegedly scientific work.

The TSB study purports to employ data on tobacco promotion and consumption for 23 OECD countries, as well as Singapore, for the period 1970-86, and for nine Eastern European countries for the period 1980-86, a total of 33 countries.[3] It then assigned a score to each country for each year according to the extent of advertising restrictions placed on tobacco promotion. Countries were then grouped into five categories: total ban for health reasons; total ban for political reasons; promotion allowed in a few media; promotion allowed in most media; and promotion allowed in all media. The average 'ban' score for each group was then calculated and trends compared in tobacco consumption and the percentage of adults who smoked in the various 'policy' groups/countries. The Report further claimed it had controlled for income level and real price changes in comparing changes in consumption and numbers of smokers.

The Report concluded that *per capita* tobacco consumption declined by 1.6 per cent per year in countries where a total ban existed, contrasted with a 1.7 per cent increase in countries where promotion was allowed in all media. The Report also alleged that the data from 20 advanced countries showed a 3.6 per cent annual average decline in adult smoking where there was a total ban, compared with a drop of 1.2 per cent in countries where tobacco

---

[2] *RJR-MacDonald, Inc. v. Attorney General of Canada*, 82 D.L.R. 4th 449 at 503 (1991).

[3] TSB Report, p. 62. Data for the Eastern European countries prior to 1980 were considered inadequate.

promotion was unrestricted.[4]

It is instructive to look at some of the more glaring deficiencies. A key criticism voiced by Professor T. D. Sterling of Simon Fraser University was that the data 'is not sourced specifically and individually in a way that would allow the data to be checked'.[5] There is a general rule amongst scholars that if the underlying data of a study cannot be employed to replicate results, the study should be totally ignored. Thus the Report claimed Portugal, as a 'total ban' country, experienced a 5.1 per cent annual decline in tobacco consumption over the years 1983-86. Yet the Canadian government's chief expert testified that more accurate information suggested the actual decline was 1.7 per cent.[6] Furthermore, there was a misclassification of Portugal as a 'total ban' country because it had an advertising restriction score lower than Sweden and identical to Italy, both of which the Report chose to characterise as countries where promotion was allowed in 'few media'. Had Portugal been characterised correctly (as a 'few media' country), the results would have shown a considerably smaller rate of decrease in the total ban countries than in countries that allowed tobacco promotion in most media. Specifically, based on the data in Table 7.5.1c of the TSB Report, the 'total ban countries' would have shown average change in smoking rates of only - 0.4 per cent, while the 'few media restrictions' countries, including Portugal, would have had an average change of - 7.6 per cent.

Moreover, countries that changed their tobacco promotion policy over time were treated differently. One example is Portugal, which is shown as being in the 'promotion allowed in all media' for the period 1970-82, and – seemingly incorrectly – as being a 'total ban' country for the years 1983-86. Similarly, Italy and France appear in two groups, reflecting their advertising restrictions at different

---

[4] Even though this conclusion cannot be given credence, as explained below, the conclusion itself acknowledges that 1.2 per cent or one-third as many adults ceased smoking in 'no restrictions' as in 'restrictions' countries. TSB suggests there is a large decline in adults who smoke quite unconnected with advertising.

[5] T.D. Sterling, 'Statistical Error in the New Zealand Toxic Board Report', in NZ Tobacco Institute, *Independent Scientific Review of the Toxic Substances Board Report*, Auckland, 1989, p. E-3.

[6] Testimony of Dr Jeffrey E. Harris in *RJR-MacDonald, Inc. v. Attorney General of Canada, op. cit.*, Vol. 63 at 9616–17 (6 June 1990).

times. Yet, the same is not true for Finland, Iceland, and Norway, all of which imposed a ban during the study period. No data are given for these countries for the period prior to the ban, yet other sources[7] indicate that the rate of decline in these countries was no greater after the ban than before it. By selectively leaving out these countries, the TSB guaranteed its results. Or, as the Canadian Superior Court said, 'the input data used ... were unreliable and [this] led necessarily to the desired results'. [8, 9]

In addition to the use of selective data, the TSB presented its data in a highly selective way. Table 1, below, from the TSB Report's Table 7.5.1a,[10] illustrates this selective use and presentation of data.

It will be seen that the large decrease in the group average annual decrease in smoking of -3.6 per cent depends on Iceland – a country with a population of approximately 300,000 persons – and relies on data for but one year (-9.5 per cent). Such data cannot be averaged unless weighted, perhaps by years of data coverage, or size of population, or some other weighting system. Moreover, this huge decrease in smoking in Iceland in 1985-86 is attributed to the advertising ban instituted in 1972. The assumption of a continuing effect on smoking habits of Icelanders in 1985-86, 13 years after the introduction of the advertising ban, is patently implausible. To suggest that the country's rate of change in smoking in 1985-86 is representative of the entire period 1972-86, would imply an impossibility – that more than 100 per cent of the population of Iceland smoked in the year in which the advertising ban was instituted.

Additionally, the TSB study did not take account of the possibility that the alleged decrease in tobacco consumption (or the number of smokers) might be due to factors quite independent of

---

[7] See J. Boddewynd (ed.), *Tobacco Advertising Bans and Consumption in 16 Countries*, New York: International Advertising Association, 1986.

[8] *RJR -MacDonald, Inc. v. Attorney General of Canada*, 127 D.L.R. 4th 1 at 60 (1995).

[9] In *RJR-MacDonald, Inc. v. Attorney General*, the Attorney-General's own expert witness admitted that data underlying the TSB Report were flawed and that he had used 'corrected' data from the NZ Dept. of Health in his testimony, although revised data were eventually furnished to the plaintiff.

[10] TSB Report, *op. cit.*, Table 7.51a at 68.

Table 1: Replication of TSB Report Data

Country and year of ban	*Years surveyed*	*Percentage who smoke*		*Annual percentage change for the country*	*Group average*
		Beginning	End		
Iceland (1972)	1985-86	40.0	36.2	- 9.5	
Finland (1978)	1978-86	25.8	25.5	- 0.1	- 3.6
Norway (1975)	1973-86	41.5	34.5	- 1.1	
Portugal (1983)	1983-84	n.a.	23.5	n.a.	

Source: TSB Report, Table 7.5.1a, p. 68.

the restrictions on advertising. It would be surprising if some (or all) of the decrease in tobacco consumption were not due to changes in social mores. The declining rate of smoking reported in the TSB Report may be no more than a continuing trend toward cessation of smoking, having nothing to do with advertising. Indeed, the very process of enacting a ban often reflects declining support for smoking and therefore is likely to be a result rather than a cause of smoking cessation.

The Laugesen and Meads (1991) Study [11]

The deficiencies of the TSB Report have been recognised not only by Canadian courts and independent researchers, but by the authors of the Report themselves.[12] Indeed, they generated new and 'corrected' data for a new study[13] intended to rectify some of the earlier errors. However their second effort suffers from basic flaws in methodology and data that renders it unintelligible and of no probative value.

---

[11] M. Laugesen and C. Meads, 'Tobacco Advertising Restrictions, Price, Income and Tobacco Consumption in OECD Countries, 1960–1986', *Brit. J. of Addiction*, Vol. 86, 1991, pp. 1,343–54.

[12] Murray Laugesen was the senior author of the TSB Report and was, at the time of the Report, a 'community medicine specialist' with the NZ Dept. of Health. Personal communication from M. Laugesen to the author, 11 December 1991.

[13] L & M., *op. cit.*

In their study Laugesen and Meads (L&M) hypothesise that tobacco consumption per adult is dependent upon a number of variables, such as the real price of tobacco products (allowing for inflation), real income *per capita*, the number of females in the work force, and the level of advertising restrictions in the countries studied. They then create a country-by-country, year-by-year advertising score for each of the 22 OECD countries in their study. Their multiple regression model predicts that consumption falls as their index of advertising restrictions rises. However, this attempt to salvage the TSB Report has been extensively criticised. Stewart[14] found the data to be flawed in significant ways. He shows that by drastically understating the sharp increase in the real price of tobacco, the fall in consumption could be unrealistically attributed to other causes, for example, the curbs on advertising.

Over and above such 'flawed data' problems, there is a more basic conceptual deficiency in their 'advertising restriction score'. To illustrate, a country has a choice of imposing: (i) a complete advertising ban; (ii) a ban on non-print media advertising; (iii) a ban on television advertising only; or (iv) no ban. Standard regression techniques can test the predictive value of each of these independent variables separately. For each variable the investigator would assign a value of either '1' or '0', according to whether the country under inquiry employed that particular policy. However, if researchers attempted to assign 'scores' of '3' to complete ban countries, '2' to partial ban countries, and '1' to no ban countries, their implicit assumption is that complete bans are three times more effective than no bans and partial bans are twice as effective, and so on. Thus the model would embody the very assumptions about those effects that it was designed to test. Only if each variable were treated separately as an independent binary (either/or) variable, would the regression be valid. By ignoring this rather basic principle of research, L&M have allowed their qualitative 'score' to enter into their regression in fully 20 different ways. This is such an egregious error that it totally invalidates their results.

---

[14] M.J. Stewart, 'Tobacco Consumption and Advertising Restrictions: A Critique of Laugesen and Meads (1991)', *Int'l. J. of Advertising*, Vol. 11, 1992, pp. 97–118.

The British Health Department Study (the 'Smee Report')[15]

Given the intense controversy over the TSB and L&M studies, the UK Department of Health undertook its own study. This report is vastly better than those reviewed above because it recognised the wide disagreement about the relationship between advertising and consumption of tobacco. However, the Henley Marketing Dynamics research group well observed:

> 'Our review concludes that the analysis undertaken in the Smee report does not justify its findings. The evidence presented is limited, its analytical approach is flawed, and the conclusions advanced are invalid. The Department of Health has not satisfactorily demonstrated that tobacco advertising has an effect on consumption, or that advertising restrictions and bans have reduced consumption where they have been applied.'[16]

Recognising the weaknesses, both methodological and statistical, of most of the earlier advertising-consumption studies, the Smee Committee determined to review the extant literature and, more importantly, to conduct their own studies on three countries (New Zealand, Canada, and Norway), as well as relying on a published study concerning Finland's experience with a ban. Most of the Report is concerned with the second weakness (statistical and econometric); much of it is highly technical and set out in two annexes to the Report.

The Henley Marketing group noted the Smee Report is divided into two basic sections: a review of the indirect and circumstantial evidence and a review of the direct evidence. The review of the indirect evidence is, in turn, divided into five distinct sections:

- the nature and incentive structure of the tobacco market;

---

[15] C. Smee *et al.*, *The Effect of Tobacco Advertising on Tobacco Consumption: A Discussion Document Reviewing the Evidence*, UK Dept. of Health, Economics and Operations Research Division, 1992, pp. 1–55. The study has come to be called the 'Smee Report' after the head of the division.

[16] Laurence W. Hagan *et al.*, *A Review of The Effect of Tobacco Advertising on Tobacco Consumption*, London: Henley Marketing Dynamics International, The Henley Centre for Forecasting, January 1993.

- mechanisms whereby consumption might be increased by advertising;
- the evidence on reactions to advertising;
- evidence from surveys of reasons for starting smoking; and, finally,
- other evidence on indirect effects.

We discuss these briefly in turn.

Smee's discussion of the nature and incentive structure of the tobacco market, begins with a fundamental error. Specifically, it suggests that the tobacco market is monopolistic and/or characterised by a high degree of collusion between tobacco manufacturers. It would follow that it 'could prove profitable for a monopolistic firm to advertise in order to expand the market for cigarettes'. This is an unexpected argument, given (a) subsequent statements Smee makes, and (b) the fierce competition in the tobacco industry which led *Marketing Week* to describe intra-industry competition as 'the vicious tobacco wars'. [17]

On 'collusion', the Smee Report itself asserts that 'there is no evidence of collusive arrangements to promote a monopoly'.[18] Indeed, the following description of the 'tobacco wars' appeared in a leading advertising magazine, following the announcement by Philip Morris that it was merging its UK sales operation with that of Rothmans.

> 'The drawn-out hostilities have left many battered and bruised, including the world's largest cigarette company, BAT Industries...I once worked for a chief executive who had Von Clauswitz's Rules of Warfare framed and displayed on his office wall, and talked of the "opposition" companies as if they had similar characteristics to those of Nazi Germany.' [19]

The authors of the Smee Report discuss the mechanisms by

---

[17] *Marketing Week*, 29 September 1989 (n.p).

[18] Smee Report, *loc. cit.*

[19] *Campaign*, 25 August 1989 (n.p).

which advertising might increase consumption. This section is entirely theoretical and is but a series of conjectures about ways advertising might encourage people, and especially young people, to smoke. In the process Smee chose to ignore a vast literature[20] which overwhelmingly suggests that people start smoking because of peer pressure and family – not because of advertising. This is a most regrettable omission from the Report.

The section on 'reactions to advertisements' summarises a number of largely academic papers suggesting that tobacco advertising affects young people. The Report concludes that, taken as a whole, the papers and studies demonstrate that young people are aware of tobacco advertisements and cigarette brands and, particularly, 'eye-catching ones' such as those involving 'Joe Camel'.

It fails, however, to consider that an awareness of a product hardly implies that the person so aware will in fact purchase the product. Indeed, this failure has a specific name in the marketing community – the 'Rosser-Reeves fallacy' – named after the advocate of the hypothesis that those who are more aware of a product are also more likely to purchase it. This principle of 'selective perception' is so well known in marketing circles, that the Institute of Practitioners in Advertising in the UK explicitly excludes such 'bootstrapped' proofs of advertising effectiveness from their annual Advertising Effectiveness Awards.

When the Report considered the evidence from surveys of why people begin smoking, it looked at only two studies, both of which, basically, commit the Rosser-Reeves fallacy. Even so, these two studies do not support the contention that there is any relationship between advertising awareness and smoking. Smee looked at a UK study[21] which found no association between awareness and approval of smoking among boys, but did find a link among girls. The other study from Australia[22] found that approval of advertising

---

[20] See Section 3.

[21] Office of Population Censuses and Surveys, *Why Children Start Smoking*, London: HMSO, 1990.

[22] H.M. Alexander, R. Callcott, A.J. Dobson, G.R. Hardes, D. M. Lloyd, D. L. O'Connell and S. R. Leeder, 'Cigarette Smoking and Drug Use in School Children', *International J. of Epidemiology*, 1983, Vol. 12, pp. 59–66.

came fourth out of five factors contributing to variations in smoking behaviour. Moreover, the Report itself acknowledged that 'it [is] possible that the causation runs in the other direction – children disposed to smoke are more likely to react positively to tobacco advertising and show greater awareness of it'. [23]

The final section of Smee on the 'indirect and circumstantial evidence' consists of but two paragraphs. One suggested that tobacco advertising may tend to induce smokers to ignore the dangers to their health, based on a 1983 survey showing that more smokers than non-smokers agreed with the statement that 'smoking can't really be dangerous or the Government would ban cigarette advertising'. As the Henley group has noted,[24] 'since smokers are likely to be favourably disposed towards smoking, particularly more so than non-smokers, this result offers little or no view as to the effect of an advertising ban'.

The second paragraph refers to a US study which suggests that coverage of articles on tobacco and health is restricted in magazines that receive revenue from tobacco companies. Yet not only are revenues from tobacco advertising incredibly small – less than 1 per cent of total advertising revenue in the UK – but editors of newspapers and magazines savour their editorial independence and are highly unlikely to be significantly affected by tobacco advertisers.

The Smee Report then turns to the 'Direct Evidence on Advertising and Consumption'. This section is basically a review of cross-sectional studies of the different levels of advertising controls across countries, studies in the fluctuations in advertising expenditures over time within a country, and, finally, 'before-and-after' studies following a ban on media advertising.

Smee states that there are only two international cross-sectional studies, those by Cox[25] and Laugesen.[26] It thereby ignores one by

---

23 Smee Report, p. 7, citing A. Marsh and J. Matheson, *Smoking Attitudes and Behaviour*, London: HMSO, 1983, n.p.

24 Hagan, *op. cit.*, p. 12.

25 H. Cox and R. Smith, 'Political Approaches to Smoking Control: A Comparative Analysis', *Applied Economics*, Vol. 16, 1981, pp. 569–82.

26 L & M, *op. cit.*

Stewart[27] (who had given his report to the Department of Health) and two international cross-section studies: they are the TSB study, discussed above, and a 1975 study by Hamilton.[28] Smee may have ignored the TSB study as incredibly inferior despite the publicity attached to it. But the other two it ignored (Stewart and Hamilton) both suggested that the net effect of advertising bans is to increase rather than decrease tobacco consumption. Stewart used yet more sophisticated statistical techniques and refined data in a further study, concluding more emphatically that advertising bans tend to lead to increases in tobacco consumption.[29] Despite this selective approach, Smee admits that:

> '...this evidence is suggestive rather than conclusive. Other factors could account for the…results. Social trends away from smoking may be stronger in the "legislative" countries. Indeed, there may be reverse causation – a stronger social trend away from smoking which shows up in a negative time trend in the regression equation may have created a climate of opinion favourable to legislative control of tobacco advertising.'[30]

This is precisely the possibility we have already discussed.

Of 19 time-series studies of the effect of advertising in the UK, USA, New Zealand, Australia and Germany, Smee alleges that 11 show a positive and statistically significant impact of advertising on tobacco consumption. There are a number of problems with Smee's conclusion and summary of these studies.

First, the Committee uncritically treated all the studies as of equal worth, implying that since 11 of the 19 studies suggest a positive impact of advertising on tobacco consumption, the weight

---

[27] That this was known to Smee *et al.* is made clear by the fact that on p. 54 of the Smee Report there is a bibliographic entry which reads: Stewart, M.J., 'Tobacco Consumption and Advertising Restrictions: A Critique of Laugesen and Meads' (1991).

[28] J. L. Hamilton, 'The Effect of Cigarette Advertising Bans on Cigarette Consumption', in J. Steinfield *et al.* (eds.), *Smoking and Health, Vol. 2: Health Consequences of Education, Cessation Activities and Governmental Action. Proceedings of the 3rd World Conference on Smoking and Health*, 1975.

[29] M.J. Stewart, 'The Effect on Tobacco Consumption of Advertising Bans in OECD Countries', *International J. of Advertising*, Vol. 12 (2), 1993, p. 155, which we discuss below.

[30] Smee Report, p. 10.

Table 2: 'Smee Report' Rankings of Statistical Significance of International Studies on Impact of Tobacco Advertising on Consumption

	Results	
Country	*Significant*	*Insignificant*
United Kingdom	3	4
United States	5	3
Other	3	1
Total	11	8

Source: Hagan, *op. cit*., p. 19.

of the evidence supports advertising bans. Before considering the varying quality of the 19 studies, we can see from Table 2 that eight failed to yield a statistically significant result, including four out of seven UK studies.

The Henley Marketing group went further by evaluating these studies on the basis of 14 key econometric and statistical criteria on the quality of the data, the model specification, and the statistical test employed, with one star given, or not, per each of the 14 different criteria. These results are reproduced in Table 3, below.[31] Several observations about the studies reviewed by Smee bear mention. *First*, on the grounds of specification of the model, and data and estimation methodology, seven studies finding a positive impact score fewer than half marks (7 out of 14 stars). *Second*, there is no study with as many as 10 'stars' which finds any significant relationship between advertising and consumption.

So far, Smee does not come out of this investigation very well. Having failed to look at studies known to it which had concluded against an effect, it failed to assess the quality of the studies reviewed.

The section of the Smee Report examining 'before' and 'after' studies of consumption in countries following a ban of advertising is no less suspect, because, whether intentional or not, the very way the alleged results are presented is misleading. Specifically, in reporting the evidence on broadcast bans from Hamilton's study of

---

[31] Hagan, *op. cit*., p.18. For a description of the Henley rating system, see Hagan, Appendix .

Table 3: Effect of Advertising on Tobacco Consumption in Smee's 19 Time-Series Studies

United Kingdom	*Reduction Associated with a Ban (per cent)*	*Dates of Data*	*No. of stars*
McGuinness et al (1975)	7.5	1957-68Q	2
Metra (1979)	*	1958-780	13
Witt et al (1981)	7.0	1955-75	3
Radar (1985)	3.5	1965-80Q	3
Godfrey (1986)	*[1]	1956-84	10
Duffy (1991)	*	1971-87Q	7
Dept. of Health (1992)	*[2]	1958-87	8
United States			
Hamilton (1972)	*	1953-70	4
Fujii (1980)	2-7	1929-73	7
Schmalansee (1972)	*	1956-67Q	8
Young (1983)	3	1929-73	7
Baltagi et al (1986)	*	1963-80	10
Bishop et al (1988)	7	1954-80	7
Seldon et al (1989)	9	1952-84	6
Other Countries			
Leeflang et al (1985)[3]	14-16	1960-75	3
Johnson (1986)[4]	*	1961-83	5
Chetwynd et al (1988)[5]	7[6]	1973-85	4
Harrison (1989)	8-12	1973-85Q	8

Notes: * = Statistically insignificant (level of significance varies but is either 5 or 10 per cent); Q = Quarterly data

1. Godfrey investigates a number of alternative models and data definitions in an attempt to improve the specification of tobacco demand models. A large number and a considerable range of results are produced.
2. These models are reviewed in the Henley study.
3. West Germany
4. Australia
5. New Zealand
6. Result using quarterly data; the result for annual data is not statistically significant.

11 countries, seven of which introduced a ban between 1948 and 1973, Smee reports the results in tabular form as depicted in Table 4-A, below.[32] This Table suggests there is a narrow margin in favour of the conclusion that a broadcasting ban decreases consumption. Such a conclusion is highly erroneous and/or misleading – whether intentionally or not. A simple re-arrangement in Table 4-B suggests an open verdict.

We do not here review, case-by-case, Smee's country studies. Suffice it to say that, given Smee's failure to take cognisance of the quality of many of the studies it reviewed, and given its selective review of the literature, coupled with the highly prejudicial manner of presentation of the results of those studies which were reviewed, it can safely be said that a disinterested scholar cannot give much weight to the Smee Report.

Table 4-A: Smee's Purported Demonstration of the Effect on Consumption of an Advertising Ban in Broadcast Media: Results from Seven Countries

	Reduction	*Increase*
Significant	1	1
Insignificant	3	2
TOTAL	4	3

Table 4-B: A Re-arrangement of Smee's Purported Demonstration of the Effect on Consumption of an Advertising Ban in Broadcast Media: Results from Seven Countries

Significant Reduction	*Insignificantly Different from zero*	*Significant Increase*
1	5	1

[32] Smee Report, p. 16.

Stewart's Studies of Tobacco Consumption and Advertising in OECD Countries

Stewart has produced among the best studies of advertising and consumption. The first[33] was a devastating critique of Laugesen and Mead for the mistakes in their data set. He also drew attention to the fundamental problem that L&M's model mis-specified the crucial variables – taste, cultural, and attitudinal variables – which are likely to vary across countries. Thus, L&M's regressions should not have employed a single constant term for all countries which incorrectly assumes that the autonomous level of tobacco consumption is the same for all societies. As Duffy has noted:

> '...this omission, in conjunction with many other problems identified by Stewart (1992, 1993a), detracts from the credibility of Laugesen and Mead's findings.'[34]

In further contributions[35] to this literature, Stewart developed from published sources a solid and consistent pooled cross-section time-series data set for 22 of the 24 OECD countries for a 27-year period, thus 'correcting' the data flaws which permeated the TSB Report and the L&M study. He then estimated a regression equation to explain the variation in *per capita* tobacco consumption in each country over time, noting that by 1990 six of the 22 countries had implemented a ban on all forms of tobacco advertising and that two analyses of the consumption data showed no negative effect on consumption. Specifically, he found that the dummy variable employed for an advertising ban was positive, which suggests:

> 'that the average effect on per capita tobacco consumption has been a small increase. This increase is not quite statistically significant, but clearly refutes the belief that advertising bans have appreciably reduced consumption.'

---

[33] M. J. Stewart, 'Tobacco Consumption and Advertising Restrictions: A Critique of Laugesen and Meads', 12 *Int'l. J. of Advertising*, 1992, pp. 97–118.

[34] M. Duffy, 'Econometric Studies of Advertising, Advertising Restrictions and Cigarette Demand: A Survey', 15 *Int'l. J. of Advertising*, 1996, pp. 1–23.

[35] M. J. Stewart, 'The Effect on Tobacco Consumption of Advertising Bans in OECD Countries', *op. cit.*

As Duffy has noted:

> 'Stewart points out that banning advertising also bans the associated health warnings, and this has a positive effect on consumption. This conclusion is essentially the same as that reached by Duffy (1994).'[36]

Conclusions on Cross-Sectional Studies of Advertising Restrictions and Tobacco Consumption

Our review of the international, cross-sectional studies on advertising restrictions and tobacco consumption leads to the conclusion that those studies which have received the greatest publicity – TSB, L&M and Smee – are highly biased and distorted. Additionally, these studies contain fatal flaws. The flaws of the TSB Report on data and methodology are so severe that it has been denounced as having 'no probative value'. The data errors in the L&M study, as well as its inherent denial of differences in tastes, cultural characteristics, etc. across countries, necessarily lead to rejection of its findings.

The Smee Report remains a decided improvement over the TSB and L&M studies, notwithstanding the highly prejudicial way in which it reports some of its results. Coupled with the highly selective choice of studies reviewed, it is difficult to attach much significance to the impartiality of the authors of such work.

Hamilton and Stewart, in sharp contrast, both find it at least possible that advertising bans actually led to an increase in tobacco consumption and both hypothesise that perhaps the bans, among other effects, lead to consumers being deprived of health warnings.[37] Stewart's work, in particular, is to be commended for painstakingly and laboriously developing a solid, consistent and corrected data set which will prove useful to other scholars in this field.

---

36 Duffy, *op. cit.*, p. 15.

37 See discussion of Stewart, above.

5. *Time-Series Studies of Advertising and Tobacco Consumption*

IF TOBACCO ADVERTISING WERE A SIGNIFICANT FACTOR which induces people to smoke, we might expect more smoking in countries which permit free commercial speech than in countries with advertising bans. In general, however, no such relationship exists. Whether measured by the percentage of smokers in a country, or by *per capita* consumption, tobacco consumption appears higher in many of the countries where advertising is prohibited than in countries where it is allowed. More importantly, in a number of countries where advertising is not prohibited, consumption among both adults and young people has been declining, while it has been increasing in some countries where advertising is prohibited.

The conclusion that advertising and total consumption are unrelated was expressed by the US Council of Economic Advisors in 1986, when it declared: 'evidence from other countries suggests that banning tobacco product advertising has not discouraged smoking.'[1]

This evidence is summarised in Table 5 by Stewart[2] which illustrates that, relative to 'non-ban' countries, most countries with an advertising ban experienced an increase in tobacco consumption after bans were imposed. He concludes:

> 'The population weighted average of all the figures in the Table is 103.3. So, as a simple matter of arithmetic, the average adult in OECD countries with a tobacco advertising ban consumed 3.3 percent more than if consumption trends in those countries had followed the rest of the OECD.'

[1] US Office of the President, *Economic Report of the President*, 1976.

[2] Stewart, 1993, *op. cit.*, p. 159.

Table 5: Consumption Trends in 'Ban' Countries Compared with 'Non-Ban' Countries

	Average Adult Consumption in Non-Ban Countries (grams)	*Index of Consumption Relative to Non-Ban Countries (Non-Ban Country Average = 100)*					
Year		*Iceland*	*Norway*	*Finland*	*Italy*	*Portugal*	*Canada*
1971	3220	100					
1972	3309	99					
1973	3407	96					
1974	3457	107					
1975	3411	104	100				
1976	3470	100	96				
1977	3397	100	97				
1978	3330	103	95	100			
1979	3383	103	101	102			
1980	3332	105	103	101			
1981	3306	111	92	96			
1982	3224	113	85	102			
1983	3139	121	88	108	100	100	
1984	3135	122	91	113	103	98	
1985	3112	110	99	104	105	98	
1986	3041	114	106	112	108	101	
1987	3004	117	108	120	102	103	
1988	2907	117	112	122	104	107	100
1989	2904	112	113	127	105	107	97
1990	2868	112	115	124	98	112	92
Average		109	100	111	104	104	95

Source: Stewart, *op. cit.*, Table 2, p. 159 (1993).

Trends in Smoking in Scandinavia

(i) Norway

Norway introduced a complete ban on cigarette advertising in 1975. While Bjartveit[3] has asserted that this has reduced tobacco

---

[3] K. Bjarveit, 'Fifteen Years of Comprehensive Legislation', in *Tobacco and Health 1990,*

consumption, he presents no evidence. For this reason, the Smee Report endeavoured to test Bjartveit's assertion, using data for the period 1964-89. However, Smee acknowledged its work was built on shaky foundations when it admitted:

> '...the model should include the relative price of tobacco, real income, advertising messages and changes in social attitudes toward smoking. Unfortunately, suitable data on advertising and social attitudes is not readily available. [Moreover], it is not possible to quantify precisely the share of the reduction (in tobacco consumption) attributable to the advertising ban itself.'[4]

More crucially, Smee failed to include a real price variable when the real price of tobacco products was fully 39 per cent higher in 1989 than in 1974. Thus when Smee concludes that the advertising ban seemingly served to dampen consumption, he is implicitly assuming that price increases do not serve to dampen demand – something which any economics student would find puzzling, to say the least.

In sum, it is difficult to disagree with the authors of studies in the *Journal of the Norwegian Medical Association* and *Psychological Reports* [5] who, in 1992, wrote:

> 'The enacted legislation does not seem to have affected either tobacco sales or number of regular smokers in Norway...The last ten years has been a period when in several other countries reports have indicated remarkable reduction in smoking. In a comparison...of prevalence in 1977-87, the USA, England, and Sweden had male prevalences from 24.0 per cent to 35.0 per cent while Norway had 41.3 per cent, and similarly for women these countries had prevalences of 26.8 per cent to 31.9 per cent compared to 33.3 per cent in Norway. The reduction in these countries during the same period was reported for men as 22.5 per cent to 25.0 per cent compared to 8.0 per cent in Norway and for women as 12.9 per cent to 18.4 per cent reduction compared to a 12.0 per cent *increase* [in Norway].'

World Conference on Tobacco and Health (Perth, W. Australia, April 1990).

4 Smee Report, p. 35.

5 K. O. Gotestam and K. G. Gotestam, 'Smoking and Attitudes Toward Smoking in Norway', 17(110) *Tiddskr Nor Lageforen*, 1990, pp. 2260–61; see also the same authors' 'Changes in Smoking Legislation, Attitudes, and Behaviour', *Psychological Reports*, Vol. 70, 1992, pp. 531–37.

(ii) Finland

In Finland tobacco product advertising has been banned completely since 1978. Additionally, in the period immediately preceding (1976-78), a number of interventions were made in the tobacco market, including prohibition on smoking in public places, forbidding the sale of tobacco products to persons under 16, compulsory health warnings on cigarette packets, and earmarking part of tobacco tax revenue for anti-smoking publicity.

A major study of the Finnish market is that by Pekurinen,[6] an academic affiliated to Finland's National Public Health Institute. He concluded that 'the price of cigarettes is the most important single determinant of the demand for tobacco products'. While this study has been held up as hard evidence of the importance of advertising in stimulating consumption, Pekurinen himself certainly did not think that advertising had an important effect because he did not include advertising expenditures in his econometric model, explaining 'the previous studies indicate that advertising has only a marginal impact on the aggregate demand for tobacco products'. Moreover, it is interesting to note that the tobacco market in Finland, like that in Norway, is characterised by a high proportion of pipe/rolling tobacco, of which consumption showed a 26 per cent *increase* after the banning of advertisements.[7]

Finally, a 1991 study published in the Finnish Medical Gazette[8] reported 'a slight [further] increase' in smoking among adult men and women between 1988 and 1990. Specifically, the authors report that daily smoking by adults increased from 35 to 36 per cent for men and from 20 to 21 per cent for women.

These findings are borne out by a 1994 report[9] by Statistics Finland for the Ministry of Social Affairs and Health, based on surveys from 1980 to 1993. One found a slight increase in the proportion of daily smokers in the overall population, rising from

---

6 M. Pekurinen, 'The Demand for Tobacco Products in Finland', *Brit. J. of Addiction*, Vol. 84, 1989, pp. 1183–92.

7 Luik, *op. cit.*, p. 29.

8 M. Paavola *et al.*, 'Research on Attitudes Toward Smoking in Finland', 46(8) *Suomen Laakarilehti*, 1991, pp. 721–24.

9 Statistics Finland, *Tobacco Statistics 1993*, Tilastokeskus, 1994.

25 per cent in 1979, the year following the advertising ban, to 27 per cent in 1993, although another survey found a slight decrease from 27 to 24 per cent.

(iii) Sweden

Tobacco advertising has been severely restricted in Sweden since 1979, but there has been no solid study of the effects on smoking among adults. As we shall see in Section 6, the studies on smoking among the young suggest a modest increase in smoking since the advertising ban.

Trends in Smoking in the United Kingdom

In addition to the Smee Report there have been seven studies of the tobacco consumption-advertising nexus in the United Kingdom, four of which have found no significant relationship. However, and as we note elsewhere,[10] mere counting of studies without regard to their quality can be most misleading. Thus, those UK studies which are more scientifically rigorous invariably illustrate little evidence of a discernible relationship. Or, as Hagan, of Henley Marketing Dynamics, has noted, one may reasonably conclude that

> '...after taking the general quality of the studies into account an objective overall view from the UK time series evidence presented by DoH [the UK Dept. of Health or Smee Report] suggests no conclusive advertising effect.'[11]

Support for that verdict can be inferred from Smee which observed:

> '...researchers using incomplete published data on advertising found an effect whereas...[those] which had access to the complete advertising data did not.' [12]

We now turn to several of the UK studies.

---

[10] See discussion of the Smee Report, above, Section 4, pp. 29-36.

[11] L. W. Hagan, *A Review of Effects of Tobacco Advertising on Tobacco Consumption by the Dept of Health*, London: Henley Marketing Dynamics International, 1993, p. 19.

[12] Smee Report, p. 14.

(i) McGuiness and Cowling

The first UK study was conducted in 1975 by McGuiness and Cowling (M&C). [13] This study employs (quite wisely) quarterly, as opposed to annual, data on consumption of cigarettes for the period 1957-68. Their model employed a sophisticated consumption function (lagged to allow for 'consumer inertia') as well as *per capita* disposable income, real prices measured at constant values, advertising and anti-smoking publicity.

The major conclusion of the M&C study was that, prior to the time of the Report of the Royal College of Physicians (1962) on smoking, the long-term elasticity of sales of cigarettes with respect to advertising was 0.28, and that after the Report it was 0.20. This technical measure implies that a ban on advertising would have reduced consumption of cigarettes by almost 30 per cent before the Report, and by 20 per cent after 1962.

This study has been subjected to a number of criticisms by a variety of authors, not surprisingly as it received the lowest 'star' rating given to any study by the Henley Marketing group, which awarded only two out of 14 possible 'stars' for quality on econometric and statistical grounds. Perhaps the most devastating criticism of M&C is that of Johnston,[14] who – in a 1980 paper – cast severe doubts on the model's specification, and on the estimation and testing procedures of M&C. Even more devastating than the inferior quality of M&C's econometric work, criticism has been made of the underlying data on consumption, population, personal disposable income and the price index for cigarettes, which were all derived from government sources. Their advertising data, in fact, relate only to television advertising audiences for the period 1958-65; and no data involving outdoor advertising, or other forms of promotion, were employed. Perhaps most importantly, as Hagan has noted:[15]

'McGuiness and Cowling employed a crude proxy for tobacco

---

[13] T. McGuiness and K. Cowling, 'Advertising and the Aggregate Demand for Cigarettes', *European Economic Review*, Vol. 6, 1975, pp. 311–28.

[14] J. Johnston, 'Advertising and the Aggregate Demand for Cigarettes: A Comment', *European Economic Review*, Vol. 14, 1980, pp. 117–25.

[15] Hagan, p. 68.

> advertising messages received by consumers based on audience data and cost-per-thousand estimates. This data, used in calculating the value of the advertising stock, was derived from an unpublished paper by McGuiness...Therefore, serious problems of measurement error could arise from the use of the McGuiness and Cowling data set.'

Given the qualitative, quantitative and methodological problems surrounding and underlying the M&C study, little credence can be placed on their results. Indeed, alternative testing by both the Metra and Henley Marketing groups[16] found elasticities which lent no support to the hypothesis that advertising significantly affects tobacco consumption. Simply put,

> 'taking account of all these detailed considerations, including the results of DoH's [the Smee Report] study itself, the balance of evidence falls against the argument that the UK studies demonstrate an advertising effect on cigarette consumption.'[17]

(ii) The Metra Study

One of the most thorough and complete studies of the tobacco-advertising relationship was that by Metra, a consulting company engaged by tobacco companies to scrutinise M&C's results. The Henley authors judged it 'one of the most comprehensive works on the demand for tobacco products in the use of data and its methodology'. [18]

In addition to more thorough econometric analysis, Metra had access to internal data on advertising provided by the tobacco industry. This use of vastly more reliable data makes the Metra study far superior to that of M&C. This study also employed quarterly, as opposed to annual, data on advertising and tobacco consumption, which not only provided a larger data set but gave a more sensitive response of consumption to 'mid-year' events, such as price changes.

In addition, Duffy has noted the study found that M&C's model had very low post-sample forecasting power and it was highly

---

[16] Metra Consulting Group, *The Relationship between Total Cigarette Advertising and Total Cigarette Consumption in the UK*, London: Metra Consulting Group, 1979; Hagan, *op. cit.*

[17] Hagan, p. 20.

[18] Hagan, p. 71.

unstable when estimated over various sub-periods.[19] Specifically, for the period 1968-87, using data from 1958 to 1968:

> 'the predicted and actual values began to diverge substantially after 1970, and from 1972 onwards the predicted values were at least 20 per cent too high and in some cases over 40 per cent too high.' [20]

In summary, Metra concluded that:

> '...analysing the cigarette market data for the whole twenty-year study period (1958 to 1978) showed that sales could be modelled to a good level of explanatory power in terms of price, income and the past value of sales. Adding advertising as an additional "explanatory" variable in fact added virtually nothing to the model's explanatory power and the relationship between sales and advertising was found to be insignificant.'[21]

Taken as a whole and summarising, we may conclude that the Metra study was a vast improvement on the M&C study and cast grave doubts on the validity of the M&C findings.

Since the Smee Report is sometimes cited for the proposition that advertising has a positive effect on the total consumption of tobacco products, it is most instructive to note precisely what the Smee Report says:

> 'For the advertising stock model, our results tend to support Metra rather than M&C or Radfar...advertising does not have a statistically significant effect in any form. This result is not an artefact...In the model treating advertising as an annual flow and allowing for effects with a time lag to emerge, advertising does have an effect on consumption [but] the effect takes a transitory form...which means that the level of consumption will respond initially to an increase in advertising, but if consumption is to remain at this new higher level advertising will have to rise by the same amount every year. This result has advertisers running ever faster to sustain an increased level of consumption. A given level of advertising, maintained from year to year, whatever its level, has no effect on consumption. If advertising were banned, consumption would fall after a lag and then quickly resume its former level; advertising does not affect consumption in the

---

[19] Duffy, *op. cit.*, p. 9.

[20] Hagan, p. 73, citing Metra at p. 31.

[21] Metra, *op. cit.* p. 66.

long run.'[22]

It becomes even more difficult to understand why Smee is cited by those who would ban tobacco advertising.

(iii) Radfar[23]

In an attempt to rehabilitate the M&C model following criticism from Metra that it was unstable over time, Radfar re-estimated the M&C model for 1965-80. However, it cannot be said that the attempted rehabilitation succeeded, for a number of reasons.

Radfar's data is highly suspect. Specifically, he included only press and TV advertising, and it is unclear whether he employed the volume of advertising or the flow of advertising messages (as employed by M&C) to calculate the value of the advertising stock, despite acknowledging that during the mid-1980s poster advertising rose to as much as 30-40 per cent of total spending. Moreover, he totally ignored other promotional activity by tobacco companies.

A technical critique would run along the following lines. Radfar's model is a log-linear model which incorporates several dummy variables and which he estimates by ordinary least squares. He alleges that in contrast to Metra's devastating attack, the M&C parameters are, in fact, stable. This conclusion is unsupported on Radfar's own findings since he presents differing results in his tables and, more importantly, his estimated value of the short-run elasticities of advertising stock range from 0.061 to 0.096, and he finds that only two of his parameters are statistically significant. Over and above that, he failed to perform either formal parameter stability tests, or tests of post-sample predictive power such as those recommended by Johnston.[24] Had he performed such tests, as did Duffy, he would have found advertising elasticities ranging from 0.15 to 'the minute value of 0.05 by the end of the sample,

---

22 Smee Report, p. 28.

23 M. Radfar, 'The Effect of Advertising on Total Consumption of Cigarettes in the UK', *European Economic Review*, Vol. 29, 1985, pp. 225–31.

24 J. Johnston, 'Advertising and the Aggregate Demand for Cigarettes: A Comment', *European Economic Review*, Vol. 14, 1980, pp. 117–25.

1980'.[25] Coupled with the fact that his estimate of price elasticity is but one-fifth of that obtained by M&C, the conclusion must be that the attempted rehabilitation of M&C by Radfar was a dismal failure.

(iv) Witt and Pass[26]

It is only for completeness that we note the thoroughly unsatisfactory Witt and Pass (W&P) study. While its major contribution is the attempt to incorporate the effect of health scares, it is subject to a number of methodological flaws, including its failure to test for simultaneity between advertising and sales, the use of annual data, and its specification which allows health scares and/or anti-smoking publicity to have an effect lasting as long as three years, while simultaneously presuming that the effect of advertising on consumption can never endure beyond one year. Not surprisingly, this enabled W&P to conclude that health scares would lower cigarette consumption by between 3.3 per cent and 6.9 per cent over a two-year period.

The W&P models were estimated by ordinary least squares from annual data, despite the well-known potential problems of autocorrelation and multicollinearity in simple time-series (for which W&P attempted no adjustments). Absent are any tests for the presence of serial correlation other than the Durbin-Watson, or tests for the significance of the estimated parameters and overall goodness of fit of the estimated equations when real advertising expenditures are forced into the model as an explanatory variable. It is difficult to disagree with the Henley Marketing Dynamics' verdict of the W&P model that 'little reliability can be placed on these estimates given the problems discussed above'.[27]

---

[25] M. Duffy, 'Econometric Studies of Advertising Restrictions and Cigarette Demand: A Survey', *International J. of Advertising*, Vol. 15, 1996, pp. 1–23 at p. 15.

[26] S. F. Witt and C. L. Pass, 'Forecasting Cigarette Consumption: the Causal Model Approach', *International J. of Social Economics*, Vol. 10, 1984, pp. 18–33.

[27] Henley, *op. cit.*, p. 77.

(v) Godfrey [28]

One of the better studies emanating from the UK is the 1986 study by Godfrey which is certainly a more impressive theoretical and statistical attempt to test a variety of general, and specific, models of advertising and tobacco consumption. Among the major flaws is her use of annual data only, and the failure to include complete data on advertising.

Much of her work is devoted to a most thorough and thoughtful consideration of the econometric and statistical problems in measuring the advertising-tobacco nexus, if any. For example, she recognises that ordinary least squares, as used by M&C, is totally inappropriate for an advertising stock variable. Similarly, she shows that only using the Durbin-Watson test for serial correlation is inadequate for W&P's 'habit' models. She criticises 'models of cigarette advertising [which assume that] advertising affects consumption but [which fail to recognise that] consumption...may influence advertising'. These are flawed because 'there are reasons to suspect this exogeneity assumption' and should there be simultaneity, estimating techniques such as ordinary least squares will give both biased and inconsistent results.

Godfrey tested 87 different models of tobacco consumption and in only nine did she find advertising had a significant impact on consumption. Further, while she tested fully 72 of these 87 models in log-linear form, she found a positive impact of advertising to be significant at the 5 per cent level in only eight cases, while her 15 different linear models yielded positive and significant results in only one.

(vi) Duffy [29]

Duffy has produced two important papers, both of which are not

---

[28] C. Godfrey, 'Price and Advertising Elasticities of the Demand for Tobacco – Some Preliminary Notes for the MRC Smoking Research Review Committee Steering Group', Working Paper, ESRC Addiction Research Centre, University of York, 1986.

[29] M. Duffy, 'Advertising and the Consumption of Tobacco and Alcoholic Drink: A System-Wide Analysis', *Scottish J. of Political Economy*, Vol. 38, 1995, pp. 369–85; M. Duffy, 'Advertising in Demand Systems for Alcoholic Drinks and Tobacco: A Comparative Study', *J. of Policy Modelling*, 1995; M. Duffy, 'Advertising and Cigarette Demand in the United Kingdom', Working Paper No. 9408, Manchester School of Management, Manchester: UMIST, 1994.

only novel but, arguably, far superior to the work of others since his investigation into the effects of advertising is performed within a system which allows for the simultaneous estimation of a system of demand equations for tobacco and other products rather than estimating the demand for tobacco products alone. That is, following the tenets of classical demand analysis, Duffy's approach is concerned with the decisions of consumers as they endeavour to allocate their consumer budgets optimally amongst a variety of products. This approach avoids the difficulties inherent in 'single equation' estimates, and thus is far superior and realistic.

In his 1991 paper Duffy employs quarterly time-series data for the period 1963-87 to estimate the advertising elasticity of demand. He concluded that 'the advertising elasticity of demand was found to be insignificantly different from zero'. [30]

In his 1995 paper Duffy extended his earlier work and examined the results in the light of his 'Rotterdam' model specification. After estimating and comparing six different types of advertising demand systems, he concluded:

> 'on the basis of this extensive study, encompassing a variety of model specifications, we cannot conclude that advertising has been a prime mover in the evolution of the pattern of product demand in the drink and tobacco sectors.'

In a highly interesting 1994 Working Paper for the University of Manchester, using quarterly data for the period 1963-92, Duffy investigated the effects of total cigarette advertising on the aggregate demand for cigarettes. He concluded that:

> 'no evidence has been found in this research to back up the view that aggregate cigarette advertising serves to expand total market demand for cigarettes. On the contrary, the results presented here suggest that the general effect, if one exists, of brand advertisements which carry prominent health warnings may have been to restrain aggregated demand for cigarettes. In other words, cigarette advertisements may paradoxically *reinforce* and disseminate the health education message through their warnings content.'[31]

---

[30] M. Duffy, 'Econometric Studies of Advertising, Advertising Restrictions and Cigarette Demand: A Survey', *International J. of Advertising*, Vol. 15, 1996, pp. 1–23 at p. 11.

[31] M. Duffy, 1994, *op. cit.*, p. 22.

The policy implications of this conclusion are significant since, clearly, bans on tobacco advertising are also bans on tobacco warnings and, to the extent such warnings serve to dampen the demand for tobacco products, advertising bans may well be expected to lead to an increase in tobacco consumption, rather than the reverse.

(vii) Henley Marketing Dynamics and The Smee Report [32]

Having discussed the UK Department of Health (Smee) Report, it is instructive to note that the results of the replication of Smee by Henley Marketing which found that 'a number of question marks hang over the suitability of the data employed' and 'a number of serious flaws in this analysis'. While much of the Report is a review of earlier studies, Smee also performed its own tests with data from Norway and the UK, using two different econometric models in each case. Having replicated the Smee reports, Henley tested its own models.

The first observation is that Henley's work was, quite properly, scathing about the underlying data used by Smee in its test of Norwegian advertising bans. Henley noted two major flaws in Smee's underlying data. *First*, the Norwegian data totally ignored the importance of hand-rolled tobacco which is cheaper and accounted for about two-thirds of cigarettes smoked in Norway.[33] Even more devastating for Smee is that the consumption data it employed were furnished by the Norwegian National Council on Tobacco and Health, an anti-smoking pressure group, despite published OECD consumption data being readily available, and which would have led to widely differing results.

A *second* major criticism was Smee's econometrics. Henley has noted that its model error terms for the Norwegian data do not at all justify the use of ordinary least squares on either theoretical or empirical grounds.[34] The Smee equations exhibit 'autoregressive conditional heteroscedasticity', implying that the variance of a disturbance may well be correlated with a preceding error. This

---

[32] Hagan, *op. cit.*

[33] Bjartveit, *op. cit.*, p. 76.

[34] Hagan, p. 38.

implies that an estimator employing multiple linear equations, might be considerably more efficient than the use of ordinary least squares.

Moreover, the fact that Smee dropped the price and income terms, on the grounds of alleged insignificance, is most disturbing since a number of other studies found them to be highly significant determinants of consumption.

A full story of the Henley Report can lead only to the conclusion that little or no credence can be placed in the Smee Report on the Norwegian data.

Smee's UK results are broadly in keeping with those of Metra and conclude there is little to support either M&C or Radar since advertising is found to have a modest, and but transitory, effect on consumption. One of Smee's more interesting findings for the UK is that consumption, lagged four quarters, has an effect on current advertising, implying that consumption affects advertising expenditures and not conversely. While better than its treatment of the Norwegian data, the Smee Report's econometric techniques, and results for the UK data, leave much to be desired.

Nevertheless, given the publicity which has been given to the Smee Report, it is well to remind the reader that Smee concluded: 'Advertising does not have a statistically significant effect in any form.'[35]

(viii) A Summary of the 'UK' Studies/Findings

Before turning to work involving other countries, it is instructive to summarise what we learn from the UK studies.

While the earlier studies of the advertising-tobacco consumption by M&C, Radfar and W&P showed some modest effects of advertising on tobacco consumption, Metra and Johnston have demonstrated that these findings are highly flawed, both in their data and, perhaps more importantly, in their econometric and statistical techniques.

In contrast, more recent studies by Metra and two by Duffy show that the effect on tobacco consumption as a result of advertising is insignificantly different from zero. Moreover, Duffy's 1994 study found a negative relationship between advertising and con-

---

[35] Smee Report, p. 140, as cited in Luik, *op. cit.*, p. 3.

sumption, suggesting most interestingly that a decrease in tobacco advertising meant a decrease in health warnings on tobacco products, which in turn might have led to an increase in tobacco consumption.

In short, the UK studies demonstrate that there is no credible evidence that advertising of tobacco products leads to increases in tobacco consumption.

Trends in Tobacco Consumption in the United States

(i) Introduction

There have been at least 13 econometric studies for the US, employing time-series data for periods extending as far back as 1929, with some employing data as recent as 1990. In general, these studies are of a high level of econometric sophistication and, using more reliable data on advertising expenditures, do not suffer from many of the deficiencies of studies from other countries.

Given the number of American studies, we confine our comments to the five receiving the highest Henley ratings of the eight they considered. We briefly comment on the Grabowski studies of 1976 and 1978 which have become landmark works in the field of industrial organisation, the 1992 Wilcox and Vacker paper which is the most recent and complete study we have been able to find for the entire US, and the 1997 paper by Hu, Sung and Keeler, because it is widely cited for the proposition that advertising does have a significant effect on smoking behaviour.

(ii) The Schmalensee Study [36]

Duffy described Schmalensee's study as marking 'the beginning of an important new era spanning two decades of scholarly, econometric investigations into the determinants of cigarette demand'.[37] Despite being almost a quarter of a century old, it is exceptionally sophisticated in its econometric treatment of the advertising-consumption relationship, and is laudable for its recognition that relative, as opposed to absolute, prices are decidedly more important determinants of demand. While

---

[36] R. Schmalensee, *The Economics of Advertising*, Amsterdam: North-Holland Press, 1972.

[37] M. Duffy, 1996, *op. cit.*, p. 2.

Schmalensee estimated fully 72 different models of demand, for periods from 1956 to 1967, using two-stage, as well as ordinary least squares equations, his models were variations of a general form in which cigarette demand is a function of current and lagged values of real income, relative price and cigarette advertising. Among his important contributions, Schmalensee early noted that the use of ordinary least squares to estimate tobacco demand was likely to bias results upward because of the likely simultaneity between sales and advertising expenditures so that as sales went up, tobacco firms would be likely to spend more on advertising.

Perhaps equally importantly, Schmalensee noted that rather than use the absolute level of tobacco advertising as a variable, we should look at the amount of advertising on tobacco products, relative to total national advertising. This fits economic theory and common sense:

> 'If all advertisers double their outlays, there is no reason to suspect a sudden shift to cigarettes. On the other hand, if cigarettes do not increase their advertising while all other industries begin spending more, one would expect cigarette sales to fall, unless advertising has no impact on cigarette sales. The analogy with the use of relative instead of absolute prices is immediate.'[38]

This recognition that in estimating the demand for tobacco products, one should also include other advertising is an important insight. As Duffy has noted, a failure to include external advertising in a model may result in '... the estimate of the elasticity of demand with respect to the included cigarette advertising [being] biased'.[39] Schmalensee's tests concluded that there was no statistically significant relationship between consumption and advertising for the period 1956-67. But despite his innovative contribution, the weakness is that he employs only annual data for 12 years.

(iii) The 1972 Hamilton Study[40]

Another early study was by Hamilton who endeavoured to predict

---

[38] Schmalensee, *op. cit.*, pp. 173–74.

[39] M. Duffy, *op. cit.*

[40] J. L. Hamilton, 'The Demand for Cigarettes: Advertising, the Health Scare and the Cigarette Advertising Ban', *Review of Econ. Statistics*, Vol. 56, 1972, pp. 401–11.

the effects of the 1971 broadcast advertising ban, as well as of other health scares and anti-smoking publicity generated under the US 'Fairness Doctrine', which ensured that company advertising in broadcast media was matched by anti-smoking messages. Using data for the period 1925-70, Hamilton found a positive but insignificant relationship between advertising and consumption. Perhaps more important was Hamilton's conclusion that a ban on advertising could result in an increase in consumption because of the removal of health warnings.

(iv) The Baltagi and Levin Study [41]

The study receiving the highest Henley rating (10 out of 14 possible stars) was the 1986 work of Baltagi and Levin (B&L). While Henley may have been generous in its assessment as measured by econometric and statistical soundness, it is certainly one of the better works.

B&L used pooled annual data from 46 states for 1963-80 to estimate a demand function for cigarettes. Among the more innovative aspects is that as one of their independent variables B&L used the real price of cigarettes in one state, and the minimum real price in neighbouring states so as to capture the effect of 'bootlegging'. Further, to capture the effects of the 'Fairness Doctrine' and the effects of the advertising ban in 1971, they employ both a *per capita* index of cigarette advertising and dummy variables for the effects of the advertising ban and anti-smoking commercials on television. Among its econometric merits, the study pooled the raw data via an error component model as well as an ordinary least squares model, and applied a Within transformation and a Hausmann-Taylor estimation procedure. Further, a Zellner-Geisel estimation procedure was used to distinguish between the lagged impact due to consumption and other effects.

Among their findings B&L found that the effects of advertising decayed quite quickly and they concluded that 'our results indicate an insignificant income elasticity for cigarette demand'. They

---

[41] B. H. Baltagi and D. Levin, 'Estimating Dynamic Demand for Cigarettes using Panel Data: The Effects of Bootlegging, Taxation and Advertising Reconsidered', *Rev. of Economics and Statistics*, Vol. 68, 1986, pp. 148–55.

concluded from the price elasticities, and the price elasticities with respect to neighbouring states, that 'as an anti-smoking tool, cigarette taxation may not be as effective in reducing cigarette consumption as previously thought'. Finally, they attempted to test Hamilton's[42] hypothesis that anti-smoking and health messages were more important in reducing consumption than promotional advertisements, and that the net effect of the advertising ban was to lead to an increase in consumption. They concluded that the impact of advertising on consumption was insignificant and the effect of the broadcast 'Fairness Doctrine' was negative, so that the sum of the two effects was not significantly positive.

(v) Bishop and Yoo [43]

The Bishop and Yoo study, published in 1986, is significant for considering not merely the demand side of the market, but also the supply side by employing simultaneous equations to estimate the US market for the period 1954-80. As independent variables their demand function employed the retail price of cigarettes, real disposable income, and advertising expenditures. Regrettably, they did not include either advertising or the price of other goods.

That said, B&Y's results suggested that the elasticity of demand with respect to advertising was positive and significant, but small, such that a 10 per cent decrease in advertising expenditures would be expected to lead to a decrease in consumption of only 0.7 per cent. This led them to conclude that:

> 'this small coefficient confirms previous...studies...which suggest that in the industry as a whole, advertising was not very effective in inducing more demand, but perhaps caused a change in intra-industry market share.'

---

[42] Hamilton, *op. cit.*

[43] J. A. Bishop and J. H. Yoo, 'Health Scares, Excise Taxes, and Advertising Bans in the Supply and Demand for Cigarettes', *Southern Economic Journal*, Vol. 52, 1986, pp. 402–11.

(vi) Fujii [44]

Of the studies which Henley rated most highly, Fujii is the only one which purports to find a positive, significant relationship between industry advertising and consumption.

It employed the same basic data set as Hamilton and concluded that 'advertising elasticities, in line with previous results, were small but positive'. Specifically, Fujii found a 10 per cent fall in advertising would lead to decreased cigarette consumption of 0.6-0.7 per cent, depending upon the choice of advertising variable.

One of the more troubling problems with Fujii's work was his employment of ridge regression techniques in an attempt to resolve the multi-collinearity problem, an econometric device potentially fraught with problems. It is not clear that the results of this technique are superior to those produced by ordinary least squares. Accordingly, while Henley quite rightly gave this study seven stars for its econometric soundness (the same as Bishop and Yoo), Fujii's results may well be upwardly biased by not allowing for simultaneity, nor including external advertising.

(vii) The Wilcox and Vacker Study[45]

Wilcox and Vacker (W&V) is especially noteworthy for the period covered (1961-90), the use of quarterly data and, in particular, for the employment of backward stepwise regression. This paper employed a number of potentially explanatory variables, which they 'stepped backward' into their regression programme, thereby eliminating those variables which were non-significant.

Uniquely, their measure of consumption was federal tax-paid factory withdrawals of small cigarettes, in millions of units, which they believed the most reliable continuous measure of cigarette sales. A difficulty is that it fails to include advertising on 'other' goods and makes no attempt to resolve the simultaneity problem that increased sales may be followed by increased advertising. They conclude that 'total advertising is not significant in either the full model or the final model'.

---

[44] E. T. Fujii, 'The Demand for Cigarettes: Further Empirical Evidence and its Applications for Public Policy', *Applied Economics*, Vol. 12, 1980, pp. 479–89.

[45] G. B. Wilcox and B. Vacker, 'Cigarette Advertising and Consumption in the United States: 1961-90', *International J. of Advertising*, Vol. 11, 1992, pp. 269–78.

(viii) The Franke Study [46]

Not unlike the W&V paper, this relatively recent contribution (1961–90) by Franke employs data derived from federal tax-paid factory withdrawals, aggregated to arrive at quarterly data which is divided by the population over 16 to arrive at consumption *per capita*. His independent variables are real *per capita* income, the price index, cigarette prices, real advertising expenditures on tobacco, but exclude external advertising, and dummy variables which endeavour to measure the effects of health reports and media policies.

His conclusion is that advertising has no significant effect on consumption.

(ix) Hu, Sung and Keeler [47]

A recent contribution is the 1995 work of Hu, Sung, and Keeler (HSK). It is a study of the effectiveness of an anti-smoking campaign by the State of California during the period 1990–93; and the counter-balancing effect, if any, of tobacco advertising. The State campaign was directed at four groups: adult smokers generally, pregnant women, ethnic minorities, and children. The anti-smoking campaign employed the print media, billboards, television and radio. HSK found that the anti-smoking campaign did have a statistically significant effect in reducing cigarette consumption. However, their Table 1 suggests that at a time when the average *per capita* annual consumption was approximately 3,800 cigarettes, for every million dollars spent on anti-smoking advertising, *per capita* consumption would fall by only 5.3 cigarettes, that is, by 0.00139 per cent per annum. This is roughly consistent with the finding of Tremblay and Tremblay[48] that advertising would serve to increase tobacco consumption by

---

[46] G. R. Franke, 'U.S. Cigarette Demand, 1961–90: Econometric Issues, Evidence and Implications', *J. Bus. Research*, Vol. 30, 1992, pp. 33–41.

[47] T. Hu, H. Sung and T.E. Keeler, 'The State Anti-smoking Campaign and the Industry Response: The Effects of Advertising on Cigarette Consumption in California', *Papers and Proceedings of the American Economics Assn.*, Vol. 85, No. 2, May 1995, pp. 85–90.

[48] C. H. Tremblay and V. J. Tremblay, 'The Impact of Cigarette Advertising on Consumer Surplus, Profit and Social Welfare', *Contemporary Economic Policy*, Vol. 12, January 1995, pp. 113–24.

approximately 3.67 cigarettes per person over 18.

In view of modest effects found by HSK and by Tremblay & Tremblay on the effects of both anti-smoking and cigarette advertising, it is surprising they are cited for the proposition that advertising has a significant effect on tobacco consumption.

(x) Summary of the US Studies

The impressive landmark study of Schmalensee in 1972 recognised that properly conducted studies should embody the tenets of the theory of consumer demand by taking account of the fact that measurement of the effects of advertising could be done only if they measure advertising on substitute and complementary products – that is, external advertising. This embodiment of orthodox consumer demand theory makes his study particularly noteworthy and sets a very high standard for subsequent researchers.

While earlier studies too often employed annual data, later studies not only used more sensitive quarterly data but also employed increasingly sophisticated econometric techniques, as indicated by the Henley rating system. Of the seven studies, five conclude that advertising has no effect on the aggregate consumption of tobacco products. The two that show some weak effect of advertising employ highly controversial econometric techniques.

Trends in Other Countries

(i) Australia [49]

In a 1986 study Johnson estimated the demand for cigarettes as a function of the price of cigarettes, the price of 'other' goods, real income, and real advertising expenditures on cigarettes, as well as dummy variables which endeavour to account for a ban on TV and radio advertising imposed in September 1976. After a number of differing regressions, he found no statistically significant effect of advertising on cigarette consumption.

Johnson's study is highly flawed since, among other things, the

---

[49] L. W. Johnson, 'Advertising Expenditure and Aggregate Demand for Cigarettes in Australia', *International J. of Advertising*, Vol. 9, 1986, pp. 45–48.

model employed is totally static. Further, he employs only ordinary least squares regression for his estimates and thereby overlooks the simultaneous determination of supply and demand. Moreover, he fails to take account of external advertising which is one of the more fundamental principles of consumer demand theory. This is particularly important, given that he relies on the highly unusual argument that consumers in Australia respond to absolute prices, and not relative prices.

Given the numerous flaws in this study (including a high degree of acknowledged autocorrelation), the negative conclusion on advertising, however suggestive, can hardly be deemed conclusive.

(ii) Germany [50, 51]

In the Smee Report, a 1985 study by Leeflang and Reuyl (L&R) was cited for the proposition that cigarette advertising serves to increase tobacco consumption. As we have seen there are a number of doubts about Smee and now L&R have pointed out that Smee misinterpreted their results. Specifically, L&R have said: 'we have strong objections against the way the outcomes of our own "classical study" are interpreted and discussed [by Smee].'

For academic journals, this is strong language, and would alone make an inquiry into the L&R studies worthwhile, even if their work were not inherently interesting.

Using good annual, bi-monthly and monthly West German data on consumption not only of cigarettes but of pipe and hand-rolled tobacco, as well as on aggregate advertising expenditures on all forms of advertising, except posters, and standard data on *per capita* incomes for the period 1960-75, the authors conclude: 'we were not able to detect a statistically significant influence of advertising on the consumption of cigarettes.'

This is one of the best designed and executed studies we have encountered, but is not without flaws, as the authors recognise. One of the more serious problems is the omission of cigarette prices and

---

[50] P. S. H. Leeflang and J. C. Reuyl, 'Advertising and Industry Sales: An Empirical Study of the West German Cigarette Market', *J. of Marketing*, Vol. 49, 1985, pp. 92–98.

[51] Also see the more recent P.S.H. Leeflang and J.C. Reuyl, 'Effects of Tobacco Advertising on Tobacco Consumption', *International Business Review*, Vol. 1, No. 1, 1995, pp. 39–54.

of consumers' expenditures from all L&R's models. Additionally, all the variables are de-trended in an attempt to reduce multi-collinearity, which necessarily means that the results are only short-run, and can be given no long-term significance. Moreover, external advertising is excluded from L&R's models so that the problem of simultaneity of advertising and sales is not resolved.

L&R concluded that the advertising elasticities are small, for example, 0.06, and that 'the influence of advertising on primary demand diminishes over time'. They added that 'we strongly disagree with the conclusion...that advertising has a positive effect on tobacco consumption'.

(iii) Greece[52]

Given the relative simplicity of this 1987 study, we mention it here only for the sake of completeness. Stavrinos attempted to discover the effect of advertising on cigarette consumption, and particularly the effectiveness of an advertising ban imposed in 1979 and eliminated in 1982. As the author did not have data on cigarette advertising for the relevant years (1970-79), he employed a dummy variable to capture the effect of such advertising and employed another dummy variable to capture the effect of the health warnings during the years 1979-82. In addition, he attempted to explain the *per capita* consumption of cigarettes as a function of a relative cigarette price index, and nominal *per capita* disposable income. Such a simple model must be treated with caution, but we may note that Stavrinos concluded that:

> 'Advertising did not have a significant effect on the demand for cigarettes and this concurs with the general view that advertising measures the intensity of inter-firm competition in an effort to increase the particular or individual share of the total demand rather than to increase the total demand itself.'

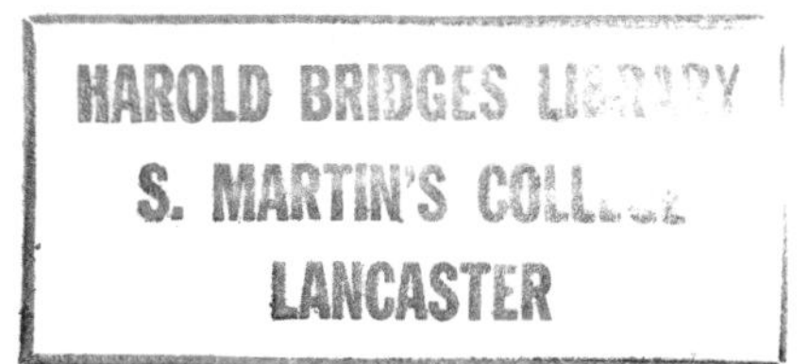

[52] V. G. Starvinos, 'The Effects of An Anti-Smoking Campaign on Cigarette Consumption: Empirical Evidence from Greece', *Applied Economics*, Vol. 19, 1987, pp. 323–29.

(iv) New Zealand – Chetwynd et al. [53]

Since the works of Laugesen and Meade/New Zealand Toxic Board study contain manifest errors, we do not here re-visit them.

In 1988, Chetwynd *et al.* attempted to test for the existence of a consumption-advertising relationship using data for 1973-85 with both annual and quarterly data on consumption and only data on print advertising for the advertising variable. The authors specified at least two forms of estimating equations: *first*, a 'habit' model in which consumption is lagged so that consumption in the current period is dependent on consumption in the recent past; and *second*, a 'carry-over' model in which the hypothesised effects of advertising in the current period are a function of a series of geometrically lagged values of advertising in earlier periods.

Among a number of strong criticisms, Jackson & Ekelund[54] and Boddewynd[55] noted that the authors failed to account for the possible/probable simultaneity of advertising and sales, the omission of external advertising, the failure to include advertising expenditures other than those on print media, and the failure to account for health scares. In addition, the econometric work was inferior, as shown by the attempt to test for autocorrelation in the data using the Durbin-Watson test, which is highly inappropriate since the authors have a lagged dependent variable. The authors note that 'the size of the regression coefficient is not large…'.[56]

Given these problems, little confidence can be placed in any of the authors' conclusions.

---

[53] J. Chetwynd, P. Cooper, R. J. Brodie and E. Wells, 'Impact of Cigarette Advertising on Aggregate Demand for Cigarettes in New Zealand', *Brit. J. of Addiction*, Vol. 83, 1988, pp. 409–14.

[54] J. D. Jackson and R. B. Ekelund, 'The Influence of Advertising on Tobacco Consumption: Some Problems with Chetwynd *et al.*'s Analysis', *Brit. J. of Addiction*, Vol. 84, 1989, pp. 1247–50.

[55] J. J. Boddewynd, 'There is no Convincing Evidence for a Relationship between Cigarette Advertising and Consumption', *Brit. J. of Addiction*, Vol. 84, 1989, pp. 1255–61.

[56] Chetwynd *et al.*, *op. cit.*, p. 413.

(v) South Korea[57]

A relatively recent (1994), interesting and novel addition to the literature is the work by Wilcox and Yang (W&Y), which deals not with the imposition of advertising bans, but their removal. Using advertising, cigarette consumption, and other data for the period July 1988 to April 1992, W&Y entered a number of variables in a stepwise regression programme to determine which variables had a significant effect on cigarette consumption. Their conclusion was that the only variables which were both positive and significant were real income and the relative price of cigarettes. Consumption was found not to be significantly affected by advertising in any of the several models tested by W&Y.

(vi) Spain[58]

Published in 1993, a study by Valdes endeavoured to measure the demand for cigarettes, and in doing so estimate the effects of advertising over the period 1964-88. Cigarette consumption is a function of real cigarette prices, real income, and real advertising expenditures, as well as dummy variables which attempt to capture the State-imposed restrictions on advertising on television and radio which existed for part of the period.

Unfortunately there are a number of weaknesses in this study, not limited to data. Specifically, Valdes did not have data for the period prior to 1973, so he extrapolated backwards from the data he did have, thus creating the same measurement error as Abedian in South Africa discussed below. Additionally, Valdes did not include data on external advertising. Coupled with the model's specification, these omissions make it of dubious validity, although Valdes suggested that:

> '…the advertising elasticity of demand for cigarettes is very low. This provides evidence to support the thesis that advertising is a weapon to divide the market but has little value for expanding industry sales.'

---

[57] G. B. Wilcox and K-T Yang, 'Cigarette Advertising and Consumption in South Korea, 1988–1992', *Internatiorial J. of Advertising*, Vol. 13, 1994, pp. 333–46.

[58] B. Valdes, 'Cigarette Consumption in Spain: Empirical Evidence and Implications for Public Health Policy', *Applied Economics*, Vol. 25, 1993, pp. 149–56.

(vii) South Africa

There are no South African studies expressly and exclusively designed to estimate the effect of advertising on tobacco consumption in South Africa. In the three studies discussed, the advertising issue is tangential to the authors' underlying investigation.

(a) Reekie[59]

In a 1992 paper Reekie hypothesised that *per capita* cigarette consumption in South Africa was a function of price, *per capita* personal disposable income, and advertising. Since his advertising data extended only from 1978 and he wished to lag advertising, he had only 12 annual observations. This, coupled with his finding that 'advertising was found to be statistically insignificant as a determinant of total market demand', led him to drop the advertising term from his final estimates. As the remainder of his work is directed to the estimation of the consumers' surplus from smoking, rather than advertising, we turn to the recent work of van Walbeek.

(b) van Walbeek[60]

In his 1996 work, van Walbeek tried to estimate the demand function for tobacco products so as to discover the extent to which the South African government might increase revenues by increasing tobacco excise taxes. While there are a number of substantial problems with this paper, we do not pursue them[61] because our interest is confined solely to the relationship of advertising and tobacco consumption.

On that issue, his verdict is negative:

> 'the most important explanatory variables of the demand for tobacco...are consumers' income, price of tobacco, past consumption

---

[59] W. D. Reekie, 'Consumer's Surplus and the Demand for Cigarettes', *Managerial and Decision Economics,* Vol. 15, 1994, pp. 223–34 (hereinafter cited as Reekie).

[60] C. P. van Walbeek, 'Excise Taxes on Tobacco: How Much Scope Does the Government Have?', *S. A. J. of Economics*, Vol. 64, 1996, pp. 20–42.

[61] The author has a *very* preliminary working paper in which some of these problems are addressed.

and population size.'

(c) Abedian/the Tobacco Control Project[62]

One of the more recent and interesting contributions to the literature for South Africa is that of Abedian, with its avowed objective of quantifying 'the extent that tobacco advertising (by suppliers) encourages cigarette consumption'. Given the publicity[63] attracted by this study, it is not unreasonable to presume that the reported result has provided anti-smoking advocates, including the project's sponsors, with useful support for their cause.

There are a number of errors in these papers, including the data which underpin Abedian's estimates of the demand for tobacco. We explore only a few here. For example, Abedian employed Reekie's data to 1989 which, earlier, Abedian and Dorrington[64] had chosen to denounce rather strongly.

Among other things, they noted that Reekie's data did not include the population of the TVBC countries, and that 'there are in fact a number of sources [for his population data, and hence his estimates of *per capita* consumption] that could have been consulted…'. It is puzzling that Abedian should employ data which Abedian and Dorrington earlier chose to denounce as highly flawed. Moreover, Abedian, having chosen data which he earlier found wanting, extrapolated it forward to produce data for the years to 1994.[65] That said, Abedian and Dorrington were quite correct: the data is flawed. Thus where Abedian shows that tobacco consumption increased from 37.89 million sticks of cigarettes in 1989 to 54.01 million in 1994 (an increase of 42.5 per cent), data

---

[62] I. Abedian, 'The Economics of Tobacco Control Project: Updates 1–3', Cape Town: University of Cape Town School of Economics Tobacco Control Project, 1995. This work, sponsored by the Canadian IDRC and the University of Cape Town, is under the direction of Prof. I. Abedian; hence hereinafter cited as Abedian.

[63] See, for example, the Cape Town *Weekend Argus*, 5/6 April 1997, p. 15.

[64] I. Abedian and R. E. Dorrington, 'An Evolution of a Recent Attempt to Assess the Social Benefits of Cigarette Smoking', *Studies in Economics and Econometrics*, Vol. 18(1), 1994, pp. 59–72.

[65] See Abedian, 'Project Update 2', p. 13, where it is asserted that 'from 1989 the 1989 value for consumption was rated forward using movements in real retail sales of cigarettes and tobacco'. It is, of course, difficult to know what this sentence means; presumptively, however, the authors mean to say, simply, that they extrapolated the Reekie Series.

are readily available from the Department of Customs and Excise which show that tobacco consumption peaked in 1991 at 40.18 million sticks, and declined to 37.45 million sticks by 1994, and to 36.54 million sticks by 1995 – a level even below that of 1988. Clearly, Abedian's extrapolation for five years served to bias his results in an upward direction. This error is more than a modest statistical artefact since one table suggests that consumption has continually increased, yet another shows *per capita* consumption peaking in 1991, and declining by 18 per cent by 1992, and still further by 1995. As Leach[66] has pointed out, population changes cannot account for the contrast between declining *per capita* consumption on the one hand, and increasing total consumption on the other.

Leach has also pointed out that Abedian's data on advertising are seriously deficient. In fact, Abedian had advertising data for only three years up to 1990 and simply estimated, by interpolation, data for 17 of the 25 years from 1970 to 1994, just as the consumption data for 1990-94 were made up by extrapolation. Little reliance can be placed on such estimates.

Finally, Abedian's quoted sources are woefully incomplete and lack the detail necessary for other researchers to replicate his work. Accordingly, it is impossible to know how much of his data is from published sources, and how much is estimated.

Abedian states several goals for his work, including identification of the principal determinants of cigarette demand and supply, estimation of the price elasticity of demand for cigarettes, and the estimation of the extent to which taxation of cigarettes affects employment in the cigarette manufacturing sector. Then there are the further goals of 'determining the impact of recent anti-tobacco advertising initiatives on decreasing tobacco consumption' and 'quantifying the extent to which tobacco advertising encourages cigarette consumption'.[67]

---

[66] D. Leach, 'Memorandum of Flaws in the Economics of Tobacco Control Project', personal communication, 14 November 1996, p. 2, and 3 February 1998.

[67] Abedian, 'Project Update # 1', August 1996, p. 1. It is interesting that Abedian's announced goal is to 'quantify the extent that tobacco advertising (by suppliers) encourages cigarette consumption'. (*Ibid.*) Stated thus, there is a presupposition that tobacco advertising does, in fact, encourage consumption.

Concentrating attention solely on Abedian's work on the advertising-consumption issue, we find he employs an econometrically sophisticated estimation technique – despite the inferior quality of the data. Specifically, he initially employs what has become known in the literature as a 'dynamic rational addiction model' which is later discarded in favour of a 'habit persistence model' where current consumption of cigarettes (like that of soap) is a function of past consumption. Such generally correct procedure, however, cannot 'save' his underlying data which, as we have seen, consist of at least one time-series in which more than two-thirds of the observations are estimated. In such circumstances, no confidence can be placed in results of even the most sophisticated econometric techniques.

Moreover, Abedian recognises that there is a 'high degree of colinearity between explanatory variables'.[68] When he includes advertising, unemployment, and the divorce rate in his estimation of the demand function, he finds such a high degree of correlation between advertising and his other variables that he is compelled to drop advertising from his final estimate of the demand function. That is, he finds that any effect of advertising on demand is swamped by the effects of income and price. More plainly, he finds advertising is not an important determinant of demand. Rather strangely for a purportedly 'neutral and scholarly' undertaking, this finding is totally ignored in his 'concluding comments'.

Having found no measurable effect of advertising on tobacco consumption in 'Project # 2', Abedian endeavours to resurrect the advertising variable in his 'Project Update # 3',[69] despite beginning with the surprisingly candid admission that, in the earlier project, 'advertising was not found to be statistically significant...'. However, he asserts that 'when the same system is estimated over the 1970-1990 period, advertising is significant at the 10 percent level'. Thus, when Abedian has actual advertising data (for the post-1990 period), he finds that advertising is not significant; when he employs data he has largely estimated (for the period up to 1990), he finds advertising is a minimally significant variable affecting cigarette consumption. Having arrived at this weak

---

68 Abedian, ' Project Update # 2', *op. cit.*, p. 4.

69 Abedian, 'Project Update # 3', *op. cit.* (October 1996).

conclusion, Abedian then determines to eschew his earlier, very sophisticated, estimation techniques in favour of a single equation model – this time for the period 1970-93, on the grounds that he discovered cointegration only during this period. When he employs this single equation model, he finds that:

> '...in this case, advertising is insignificantly different from zero. However, if the same equation is estimated over the 1970-1990 period, advertising is significant.'

It is difficult to know what to say about results which vary dramatically according to selection of data. When Abedian considers the entire period 1970-94, he can show advertising does not significantly affect tobacco consumption; when he looks at the period 1970-93 (which contains a large quantity of data he has estimated, plus some published data) his equations again yield results showing advertising is not significant. It is only when he chooses the period 1970-90, containing rather more data which he has estimated, that he gets results suggesting advertising might have a significant effect on tobacco consumption. It is difficult to know how all this can be taken seriously. Abedian's verdict hardly justifies any more extravagant claims: 'based on the results, there is some ambiguity as to the effect of cigarette advertising on the demand for cigarettes.'

Abedian then turns to the effects of anti-tobacco advertising and employs a dummy variable to account for the anti-tobacco advertising shown in cinemas during the periods 1990-92 and 1995.[70] The use of the dummy variable is to detect any consumption decreases during the period which are not captured by the other variables. The (erroneous[71]) Abedian data suggest a sharp (18.1 per cent) decrease in consumption between 1991 and 1992 which Abedian thinks is due to the anti-tobacco advertising. This claim will not bear scrutiny in view of other influences which may well have contributed to the decrease in consumption, including a

---

[70] It is difficult to understand why Abedian made this observation since, in all events, his estimation period does not include 1995.

[71] Leach, *op. cit.* Leach has informed me that the correct consumption figure for 1991 is 40,176 million sticks and that for 1992 it is 39,243 million. His source is the Dept. of Customs and Excise of the Ministry of Finance.

change in tastes. The claim is even more dubious in the light of the earlier Abedian/Dorrington comment that 'it is our contention that Reekie has not made "appropriate allowances" for "all the important influences".'[72] Abedian's suggestion that the alleged decline is attributable to the anti-tobacco campaign is not, and cannot be, supported. Suggestions to the contrary are more journalistic than scholarly.

Finally, in his conclusion, Abedian chooses to ignore his quite correct earlier observation and disclaimer on anti-tobacco advertising that '...the low number of available observations on anti-tobacco advertising limits the use of econometric techniques to quantify its effects'. Instead, he boldly asserts that '...it appears that advertising expenditure by cigarette companies does play a role in generating additional cigarette consumption'.[73]

Summarising the South African studies, we may note that there are three recent works on the effects of advertising on tobacco consumption – those of Reekie, van Walbeek, and Abedian. As we have seen, each of them expressly states that advertising has no discernible effect on tobacco consumption. Like the consistent, solid, and universal findings from other countries, none provides justification for curbs to be imposed on commercial free speech.

(viii) Summary of 'Other' Country Studies

Our examination of the available literature from 'other countries' reveals precisely the same results as do studies from the US and UK: there is no evidence that advertising of tobacco products leads to an increase in the total consumption of tobacco. These findings are not surprising, but completely consistent with (a) economic theory, (b) cross-section studies in a variety of countries, such as the work of Stewart, and (c) studies from the US and UK.

The quality of the 'other country' studies, and their supporting data, varies widely: data from Germany are exceptionally good, while those from Greece are of dubious validity. Similarly, the econometric and statistical techniques used in these studies, like the research designs employed, also vary widely. Studies such as that of Leeflang and Reuyl are very carefully crafted; others, such

---

[72] Abedian and Dorrington, *op. cit.*, p. 66.

[73] Abedian, 'Project # 3', p. 4.

as that of Chetwynd *et al.* not only have underlying data difficulties, but are riddled with econometric and statistical problems.

That said, taken as a whole, these studies – like those from the US and UK – suggest that advertising of tobacco products simply does not lead to increases in the total consumption of tobacco. Moreover, 'advertising bans' do not appear to have any significant effect on the total consumption of tobacco. This is also at one with common sense, which suggests that people simply do not alter the quantity of tobacco they purchase in response to advertising, just as people do not alter the quantity of soap they consume in response to advertising. Those who would ban advertising of tobacco products have not demonstrated that it has any effect on the total consumption of tobacco.

6. Children and Advertising

Introduction

A RATIONALE COMMONLY ADVANCED for regulating tobacco products is that smoking among the young is increased by advertising. While our concern here is not with trends in youth smoking, it is instructive to note that, as Peter van Doren[1] has recently demonstrated, short-term trends in behaviour often mask longer term trends and give the appearance that youth smoking rates have changed. This illustrates the perils of focusing attention on short- run periods. When viewed over longer periods, 'the data demonstrates that the trend in youth smoking is rather benign' and that 'the alarmist view of smoking behaviour by minors is not consistent with the data over the last twenty years'.

Despite this important finding, it is frequently argued by advocates of advertising bans that even if advertising has little or no effect on consumption by adults, children are rather more impressionable and thus more likely to be affected by advertising. There are a number of problems with this argument. Advertising bans designed to protect children also deprive adults of the right to consume/enjoy commercial speech in the form of advertising which in turn precludes them from making informed decisions on tobacco products. Further, as we saw in Section 3, advertising restrictions make it difficult for new firms to enter the market, and thus deprive consumers of new and possibly more beneficial products, including lower tar/nicotine products. Moreover, a ban on advertising removes the incentive for established producers to develop such products as a response to competitive pressures, and thus discourages innovation in the market for tobacco products.

Leaving these and related arguments aside, there are a number of good reasons against advertising restrictions designed to protect children. An immense amount of evidence contradicts the surmise

---

[1] Peter van Doren, 'Trends in Youth Smoking', *Regulation*, Summer 1997, pp. 65–68.

that people generally, and children particularly, begin consuming tobacco products as a result of advertising. Research demonstrates that the most important determinants of initiation into smoking are: (a) whether members of the family smoke, and (b) whether peers smoke.

Advocates of restrictions are fond of pointing to studies showing that children are aware of various tobacco adverts, most prominently 'Joe Camel' and 'the Marlboro man'. Yet, as we have seen, awareness hardly implies that the viewer will consume the product advertised, which would mean that advertisers have an automatic sales machine. The idea that consumers generally, and children in particular, are 'puppets of Madison Avenue' has no foundation in fact, despite the populist tirade of authors, such as John Kenneth Galbraith and Vance Packard. Serious academics in marketing and economics give such arguments little or no credence.

As we have seen, there are various reasons why some people are more aware of particular advertisements than others; the existence of 'selective perception' is well known in both psychology and marketing. As we shall see, there is ample evidence that children who are aware of advertising: (a) typically have family members who smoke, and (b) typically assert that, while aware of advertising, they have no intention of beginning to smoke. Perception is not consumption.

Without prejudging the health/medical arguments on smoking, tobacco companies are universally in the forefront of wishing to stop cigarettes being sold illegally to minors. It is at least likely that a ban would lead to a weakening of the effort to enforce the law against under-age smoking.

The Influence of Peers and Family

Family and friends are the major influences on smoking by the young. This has been widely acknowledged by governmental and university researchers around the globe. Indeed, it has been acknowledged by anti-smoking advocates, including evidence based on American Cancer Society data which concluded in 1969 from the available evidence that:

> 'Where parents or other frequently seen adults smoke, youngsters are more likely to take up the habit...Most influential of all seem to be

friends.'[2]

This view was upheld in 1983 by the Director of the US National Institute of Child Health and Human Development in evidence given to the US House of Representatives:

> 'The most forceful determinants of smoking [by young people] are parents, peers, and older siblings. If one parent smokes, the child is twice as likely to smoke as one reared in a non-smoking household. If both parents smoke, the chances become four to one. If the child's best friend smokes, there is a 90 percent probability that the child will smoke too.'[3]

Likewise the Canadian Minister of National Health and Welfare, Monique Begin, told the World Conference on Smoking and Health that 'the people who most influence a child to start smoking are his or her friends and family'.[4] This view is supported by the findings, in the same year, of Dr M. J. Ashley of the University of Toronto,[5] and by T. E. Moore, also of Toronto, in 1984.[6]

These results were certainly not confined to Canada. In studies carried out in Norway in 1975 and 1980, it was shown that where both parents smoked, and permitted their children to smoke, approximately 67 per cent of the 15-year old boys and 78 per cent of girls were daily smokers. Where neither parent smoked, and the children were forbidden by parents to smoke, the comparable

---

[2] US Congress, *Advertising of Tobacco Products: Hearings Before the Subcommittee on Health and the Environment of the House Comm. on Energy and Commerce*, 99th Cong., 1st Sess. 683 (1986).[Statement of Prof. Scott Ward on data gathered for the American Cancer Society.]

[3] US Congress, House of Representatives. *Smoking Prevention Act: Hearings on H.R. 1824 Before the House Comm. on Energy and Commerce*, 98th Cong., 1st Sess. 53 (1983). [Statement of Mortimer B. Lipsett, M.D.]

[4] M. Begin, 'Address to the Fifth World Conference on Smoking and Health', *Proceedings of the 5th World Conference on Smoking and Health*, Vol. I, p. 26 (Winnipeg, Canada, 1983).

[5] M. J. Ashley, 'Smoking and Women', *Proceedings of the 5th World Conference on Smoking and Health*, Vol. I, 1983, pp. 7, 18.

[6] T. E. Moore, *Antecedents of Smoking Onset in Children and Adolescents: A Review*, Dept. of Psychology, Glendon College, York University, Toronto, pp. 19–22 (pri. 2, 1987) quoting A. L. McAlister, J. A. Korosnick, and M. A. Milburn, 'Cause of Adolescent Cigarette Smoking: Tests of a Structural Equation Model', 47 *Soc. Psychol. Q*, 1984, pp. 24–36.

figures fell to 9 per cent for boys and 11 per cent for girls.[7] Studies of British youth in 1991 and 1992 likewise found that the roles of parents and family were the keys to juvenile smoking decisions.[8] A 1995 study published by the UK Department of Health on smoking prevalence among adolescents found that the influence of siblings was even more important than the smoking habits of parents. This same survey found that 75 per cent of adolescents who were regular smokers said that all or most of their friends smoked.[9]

The same year, a study of smoking behaviour among more than 700 urban New Zealand children, who had been tracked from birth, found peer groups were the principal link to experimentation with smoking at age 16 or above.[10]

Similarly, a 1988 study of Japanese youth found that an individual's smoking behaviour was 'most strongly related' to peer pressure. Likewise, a 1995 study of South Korean youth concluded that 'perceived peer use was the strongest predictor of cigarette smoking for boys and girls'.[11]

The influence of family smoking habits was clearly revealed in a 1990 study for the Hong Kong government which concluded that youthful smoking 'is significantly related to family smoking habits'. The study noted that, in Eastern societies where much parental supervision is exercised by female family members, there was a greater disposition by youth to smoke where mothers and/or sisters also smoked.[12] The influence of peers was held to be the

---

[7] A. Hauknes *et al.*, 'Planning, Development, and Evaluation of a Special Smoking and Health Program for Pupils Aged 12–13', *Proceedings of the 5th World Conference on Smoking and Health*, Vol. I, 1983, p. 722.

[8] E. Goddard, 'Why Children Start Smoking', *Brit. J. of Addiction*, Vol. 87 (1), 1992, pp. 17–25; and M. Isohanni, I. Moilanen, and P. Rantakallio, 'Determinants of Teenage Smoking, with Special Reference to Non-Standard Family Background', *Brit. J. of Addiction*, Vol. 86, 1991, pp. 391–98.

[9] UK Dept. of Health, Office of Population, Census and Surveys, *Smoking Among Secondary Schoolchildren in 1994*, 1995, pp. 13–14 and pp. 31–33.

[10] D. M. Fergusson *et al.*, 'The Role of Peer Affiliations, Social Family and Individual Factors in Continuities in Cigarette Smoking between Childhood and Adolescence', *Addiction*, Vol. 90, 1995, pp. 647–59.

[11] H. Juon, Y. Shin, and J. Nan, 'Cigarette Smoking Among Korean Adolescents: Prevalence and Correlates', *Adolescence*, Vol. 30 (119), Fall 1995, pp. 631–42, 637.

[12] A. B. Herts, 'Smoking Among Junior Secondary School Children in Hong Kong in 1990',

principal reason for youth smoking in a 1994 study of adolescents in Australia. The study reported that:

> 'the primary motivation to take up smoking and to keep smoking through the school years, is primarily social definition – peer identity ('where I fit in'), self-image ('who I am'), and acquiring power ('defiance /rebellion).'[13]

Research from the United States confirms the over-riding importance of peers and family in the decision by youth to smoke. A 1995 survey of youth smoking led one researcher to say that he found it:

> 'surprising that national health lobbies and officials recently downplayed parental smoking as a promoter of youth smoking' since, in the L.A. survey, 60 per cent of young smokers 'came from the minority of the households which contained a smoking parent'.[14]

He added that, given the universal exposure to advertising:

> 'it is unlikely...that this factor would explain much, if any, of the variance in youth smoking unexplained by parental smoking.'

Thus, he concluded that, as a matter of public policy:

> 'the increasing politicisation of national health policies should not mislead health educators...[to ignore] the reality that the biggest influences on, and most accurate predictors of, youth behaviour, including smoking, remain the behaviour of parents and other adults around them.'

Young people themselves invariably confirm this, as noted by a 1994 survey in Florida.[15] One of the most interesting findings comes from the focus groups which the US Food and Drug Administration (FDA) set up in the hope of supporting further restrictions on tobacco advertising. The result was to confirm that the principal reason for starting smoking was peer pressure.[16]

Hong Kong Council on Smoking and Health, 1990, p. 17.

[13] Open Mind Research Group, *National Drug Strategy – Adolescent Smoking (Qualitative Research Report)*, 27 June 1994.

[14] M. Males, 'The Influence of Parental Smoking on Youth Smoking: Is the Recent Downplaying Justified?', *J. Sch. Health*, Vol. 65(6), August 1995, pp. 228–31.

[15] D. Steinle, 'Why did They Start? To Join In', St. Petersburg *Times*, 31 March 1992, p. 2.

[16] 60 *Federal Register*, 61,673 (1 December 1995).

Finally, a 1991 study of 11-15-year-olds in the European Community found that across cultures there were consistent influences on smoking. The most significant influence was peer group, followed by family environment, interaction with friends, schooling and a host of other factors. Advertising was reported to play a role in smoking in only one-third of the countries surveyed and even then its influence was found to be far behind peer and family influence.[17]

It can hardly be doubted any longer that peers and family are far and away the overwhelming reason why youths take up smoking. It is a deliberate diversion for public health officials and/or parents to attribute youth smoking to advertising.

Studies of the Influence of Family and Friends on Youth Smoking

(1) Cross Country Research by the World Health Organisation

That family and friends are the most important influence on youth smoking was clearly established by a four-country survey conducted by the World Health Organisation in 1983-84 and published in 1986 as 'Health Behaviour in Schoolchildren'.[18] This study found that 'when young people start smoking, the most important predictor is the smoking behaviour and smoking-related activities of "significant others".' Specifically, the 'strongest statistical relationships are found with the smoking habits of the best friend', while smoking by school children is 'strongly related to the number of smokers in the family'. Most crushing for the advertising prohibitionists, WHO concluded that there were 'no systematic differences' between the smoking behaviour of young people in countries where advertising was completely banned, and in countries where it was not.

The overwhelming influence of family and friends, and the

---

[17] J. Rabier, 'Young Europeans and Tobacco: A Sample Survey of 11- to 15-year-olds in the Member States of the European Community', *The 44th E.S.O.N.A.R. Marketing Research Congress*, Luxembourg, 1991, pp. 363–87, 380–83.

[18] L. Aaro *et al.*, 'Health Behaviour in Schoolchildren: A WHO Cross-National Survey', *Health Promotion*, Vol. 1(1), May 1986.

insignificance of advertising were re-affirmed in 1991 in an update of the 1983-84 study conducted three years later and reported to the 7th World Conference on Tobacco and Health.[19] It revealed that, in general, countries with the highest incidence of youth smoking were those in which tobacco advertising was banned, while those countries which permitted tobacco advertising had the lowest incidence. For example, in Finland, where advertising had been banned for a decade, 29 per cent of the 15-16-year-old boys, and 20 per cent of girls were daily smokers. Similarly in Norway, where advertising had also been banned for at least 10 years, 16 per cent of the 15-16-year-old boys, and 17 per cent of girls of the same age, were daily smokers in 1986-87.

In contrast, in both Austria and Switzerland, where tobacco advertising was permitted, the incidence of youth smoking was significantly less – between 10 and 13 per cent.

The WHO results clearly support the view of van Raaij that:

> 'cross-national studies on smoking indicate that the prevalence of smoking is high in countries with an almost complete ban on tobacco advertising (Australia, Canada, Norway and Sweden) and low in countries with a more liberal advertising climate (Argentina, Hong Kong, Japan, Kenya, and the Philippines).'[20]

This indicates that any reinforcing and justifying effect of advertising does not cause adolescents to start smoking.

(2) The Scandinavian Experience

(a) Finland

Following the tobacco advertising ban in 1978, the incidence of youth smoking rose whereas before 1978 it had been falling. Specifically, after declining decisively prior to the ban, the incidence of smoking by 12-18-year-olds stabilised in the years

---

[19] J. van Reek, H. Adriaanse and L. Aaro, 'Smoking by Schoolchildren in Eleven European Countries', in B. Duroton and K. Jamrozik (eds.), *Proceedings of the 7th World Conference on Tobacco and Health*, Perth, 1991.

[20] W. F. van Raaij, 'The Effect of Marketing Communication on the Initiation of Juvenile Smoking', *International J. of Advertising*, Vol. 12, 1990, pp. 31–32.

1979-85 and thereafter rose,[21] with the greatest increase among girls aged 16-18, rising from 25 per cent in 1979-85 to 32 per cent in 1985-87. This trend continued. Researchers reported in 1992 that 'it has been found that...smoking...[has] increased among teenagers in Finland since the mid-1980's'.[22]

(b) Sweden

The results from Finland were mirrored by those from Sweden. Before the advertising restrictions in 1979 youth smoking had declined, according to the Swedish Board of Health, from 40 per cent in 1971 to 20 per cent in 1979 among male 16-year-olds. After the restrictions the incidence of smoking rose to at least 23 per cent by 1982. After 1984 anti-tobacco researchers acknowledged in 1990 that the incidence of youth smoking began to rise.[23]

(c) Norway

The results from Norway, where tobacco advertising was banned in 1975, suggest a somewhat similar trend. Tobacco consumption by youth had already peaked in 1974 – the year prior to the advertising ban.[24] The evidence suggests that the incidence of daily smoking among Norwegian adults (defined as those aged 15 and over) increased from 43 per cent to 48 per cent between 1979 and 1989.[25] In contrast, evidence published in the Journal of the Norwegian Medical Association suggests that the incidence of smoking among adults remained virtually constant between 1979 and 1989. Yet whether adult smoking rose or remained constant, if juvenile smoking had fallen since 1975, we would expect adult incidence

---

[21] M. Rimpela *et al., Changes in Adolescents' Health Habits 1977–1987: Preliminary Report to the National Board of Health*, May 1987, p. 2.

[22] O. Rahkonen, M.A. Berg, and P. Puska, 'The Development of Smoking in Finland from 1978 to 1990', *Brit. J. of Addiction*, Vol. 87(1), 1992, pp. 103, 108.

[23] L. Silfverforsen, A. Nygren, and G. Bolinda, 'The Swedish Society of Medicine's and the Folksam Group's Action Programme Against the Use of Tobacco', *7th World Conference on Smoking and Health*, Perth, 1991, p. 324.

[24] K. Bjartveit, 'Fifteen Years of Comprehensive Legislation: Results and Conclusions', *7th World Conference on Tobacco and Health*, Perth, 1991, p. 74.

[25] K. O. Gotesam and K. G. Gotesam, 'Smoking and Attitudes Toward Smoking in Norway', *Tiddskr Nor Laegeforen*, Vol. 17 (110), 1990, pp. 2,260–61.

also to have fallen by corresponding amounts as youth grew into adulthood. Since this did not happen, it is difficult to disagree with the conclusion by Norwegian researchers that:

> 'Even though the law to stop tobacco advertising has a meaningful content, we cannot see that it has had a fundamental effect upon the sale or use of tobacco.'

(3) US Evidence

Evidence from the United States supports the conclusions that family and friends most affect the decision by youth to smoke, and that advertising has an insignificant effect. In Congressional Hearings in 1986 an author of one of the more widely used marketing texts testified:

> 'From his parents a child acquires basic attitudes toward smoking. The more the parents smoke, the more likely the child will smoke; the more the parents discourage smoking the less likely the child will smoke.'[26]

Further, 'Friends also play a significant role in the youngster's decision to try smoking and become a smoker.' Moreover, the image children have of smokers importantly affects their decision to smoke; and children do not have a very positive image of smokers. Specifically:

> 'Children report a distinct image of the stereotypical smoker, and it is not the flattering image that anti-tobacco advocates attribute to cigarette advertising. The stereotypical smoker is viewed by children as less educationally successful, less healthy, and "tougher" than the stereotypical non-smoker.'

This necessarily led to the conclusion that:

> 'None of the research suggests that advertising influences children to view smoking in a positive light...To the contrary, the research that is available revealed in young people scepticism and distaste for cigarette advertising.'

---

[26] US Congress, House of Representatives, *Advertising of Tobacco Products: Hearings before the Subcomm. on Heath and the Environment of the House Comm. on Energy and Commerce*, 99th Cong., 2d Sess, pp. 7–8–740 (1986) at 708.

More recently, a 1993 study[27] of the determinants of teenage smoking, by J. Howard Beales of George Washington University, used two large sets of US government data to reach the same conclusions. After analysing data on more than 5,000 young people between 12 and 17, and on almost 10,000 aged 11-19, Beales concluded that:

> 'the most important variables determining teenage smoking behaviour are those reflecting the behaviour of peers. Teens are more likely to smoke if most of their acquaintances smoke, and more likely to smoke if more of their best friends smoke'.[28]

After analysing the effect both of total industry advertising and of expenditures on the most popular brands, he concluded that:

> 'The data are consistent with the hypothesis that advertising expenditures have no influence on teenage decisions about smoking. They cannot, of course, prove that hypothesis. Certainly, however, the data provide no evidence to support the notion that advertising has an important or powerful effect on teenagers' decisions.'

Advertising Awareness and the Alleged Inducement to Smoke

It is widely argued by many anti-tobacco advocates, including the US FDA,[29] that advertising is so effective in inducing children to smoke that there is a compelling case for regulation to protect those 'of tender years'. The evidence is simply lacking. Indeed, there is solid evidence that young people so discount tobacco advertising that it does not affect their disposition to smoke. It is instructive once more to consider the evidence.

---

[27] J. H. Beales, *Advertising and the Determinants of Teenage Smoking Behavior*, 1993, as cited in 'Comments before the U.S. Food and Drug Administration', Vol. 7, Docket No. 95N-0253 and 95N-0253J, 1995, pp. 46-47.

[28] J. H. Beales, *ibid.*

[29] See 60 US *Federal Register*, 41,332 (1995).

(1) The Institute of Medicine Report[30]

One authority often cited to support a causal relationship between advertising and the decision to smoke is the 1990 Report of the Institute of Medicine (IOM).

A careful reading, however, demonstrates that at no time does the IOM argue that advertising *causes* young people to smoke. All it argues is that research illustrates that 'young people who maintain an interest in smoking retain more information from cigarette ads'. Moreover, the IOM recognises that 'the effect of advertising is complex, and measuring the relative magnitude of any one type of influence...is difficult'.

It is often overlooked by those who cite the IOM report to support restrictions on advertising, that it describes as a 'questionable leap' research which purports to show a causal link between consumption and exposure to advertising or recognition of advertisements. Indeed, the IOM says:

> 'it is not known at present...whether youths already interested in smoking become more attentive to advertisements or whether advertisements lead youths to become more interested in smoking.'

In other words, the simultaneity problem precludes knowledge of whether advertising induces teenagers to smoke. Nor does the IOM Report indicate that young people are influenced by cigarette advertising. Rather, it says:

> 'several studies have shown a positive correlation between adolescents' ability to recall a particular advertisement, logo, or brand insignia and smoking intent, initiation, or level of smoking.'

It does not follow that *recall* of advertising is equivalent to *desire* or *decision* to consume tobacco products.

Other evidence frequently cited is a 1992 Gallup survey of teenagers in the United States[31] which found that over 50 per cent of all adolescents could identify the brand name associated with one of four cigarette slogans and approaching 90 per cent could

---

[30] Institute of Medicine, *op. cit.*

[31] The George H. Gallup International Institute, *Teenage Attitudes and Behavior Concerning Tobacco – Report of the Findings*, 1992.

recall seeing one or more cigarette advertisements. Again, the mere fact that a youngster recognises brands does not demonstrate that advertising causing smoking. To argue that recognition of advertising causes brand purchases is of course to 'bootstrap' the assumptions into a conclusion. This is hardly rigorous logic!

Yet although IOM recognises there is no evidence to demonstrate that advertising causes young people to smoke, it nonetheless argues for an advertising ban by invoking the unsupported assumption that there is a 'natural tendency for advertising to encourage young people to smoke'. This is not science, nor logic. It is no more than unsupported assertion.

(2) The US Surgeon General's Report of 1994[32]

Another oft-cited report is the 1994 Surgeon General's Report. As its staff is small, the Surgeon General's office does not conduct original research but merely reviews research by others. Thus in its 1994 Report, after reviewing a number of studies of advertising recall, advertising recognition and self-reported advertising exposure, it concluded that these studies demonstrate that 'young people are aware of, and respond to, cigarette advertising'. This was not only an immense leap of logic, but an error, since the studies cited show young people are aware of advertising, but they do not show that young people respond to those advertisements. In short, the simple fact is that none of the studies cited by the Surgeon General provides any evidence that advertising influences young people (or any others) to smoke. It cannot reasonably be argued that consciousness of cigarette advertising is 'harmful' or 'an inducement to smoke'.

(3) The FDA[33]

In 1995 the US Food and Drug Administration (FDA) proposed to regulate the sale of tobacco products, which would extend to regulating and/or banning advertising. In support it cited a number

---

[32] US Public Health Service, Dept. of Health and Human Services, *Preventing Tobacco Use Among Young People: A Report of the Surgeon General*, Washington, D.C., 1994.

[33] 60 US *Federal Register*, 41,332 (1995).

of studies which it claimed demonstrated a causal relationship between youth smoking and advertising. Many of these studies are also cited in the IOM and Surgeon General's Report and are discussed below.[34]

The FDA followed the IOM and Surgeon General's Reports by implying causation when none is proved. Awareness is not consumption as – presumptively – even the FDA's researchers realise.

Nonetheless, it is useful to consider the studies cited by all three agencies and to consider the issues of advertising awareness, advertising recall, and advertising recognition.

(a) Chapman and Fitzgerald – Australia[35]

In 1980 Chapman and Fitzgerald conducted a survey of almost 1,200 secondary school students in Sydney, to ascertain the relationship between advertising awareness and smoking among young people. Defining a smoker as someone who has 'smoked within the last four weeks', Chapman and Fitzgerald purport to conclude that: (a) 7th and 8th grade students who smoked were approximately twice as likely as non-smokers of the same age to be able to identify cigarette advertisements and slogans; (b) 'heavy' smokers were more likely to prefer a specific brand of cigarette than 'non-heavy' smokers; and (c) there was no ascertainable relationship between ad recognition by participants and use of recognised brands.

Chapman and Fitzgerald is a very thin reed on which to support public policy on advertising since it is a highly flawed study. The correlation between smoking status and ad recognition is still far from illustrating any causal relationship. Indeed, one would expect smokers to pay more attention to advertisements than non-smokers so that it would be surprising only if the survey found no correlation. Furthermore, Chapman and Fitzgerald employed a highly non-representative sample of the underlying population, over-representing females and 8th graders, while under-

---

[34] The proposed regulations are presently under judicial review.

[35] S. Chapman and B. Fitzgerald, 'Brand Preference and Advertising Recall in Adolescent Smokers: Some Implications for Health Promotion', *Am. J. Publ. Health*, Vol. 72, 1982, p. 491.

representing males and 7th graders. An additional sampling problem, for which the authors did not allow, was that the number surveyed within each school was a function of individual teacher willingness to participate in the survey. Thus they acknowledged:

> 'any conclusions arising from the study may not warrant generalization to school children at large but to school children with teachers interested in running such a...program.'

(b) Aitken et al.[36]

Another study cited by the FDA was conducted among almost 850 adolescents between the ages of 11 and 14 by Aitken and Eadie in 1988 in Glasgow, Scotland. This study did, in fact, find a correlation between smoking by underage youth and ad recognition, but the authors fully acknowledged such a relationship

> 'does not necessarily mean that advertising plays an important part in inducing children to start smoking. Cause-and-effect relationships are always difficult to disentangle. For example, children may become more aware and appreciative of cigarette advertising after they start smoking.'

Aitken *et al.* conducted a follow-up survey with 640 of the 850 students one year later. The purpose was to examine changes in the students' intentions to smoke when older by measures of cigarette perception. As in the first survey, students were asked 'Do you think you will smoke cigarettes when you are older?' The results were so confused and the interpretations of changes so flawed that they can provide no support for the argument that advertising induces schoolchildren to smoke.

(c) O'Connell[37]

Yet another study cited by the FDA and anti-tobacco advocates in support of advertising bans is that of O'Connell *et al.*, published in

---

[36] P. P. Aitken and D. R. Eadie, 'Reinforcing Effects of Cigarette Advertising on Under-Age Smoking', *Brit. J. of Addiction*, Vol. 85, 1990, pp. 399–412. Also, P. P. Aitken *et al.*, 'Predisposing Effects of Cigarette Advertising on Children's Intentions to Smoke When Older', *Brit. J. of Addiction*, Vol. 86, 1991, pp. 383–90.

[37] D. L. O'Connell *et al.*, 'Cigarette Smoking and Drug Use in School Children: II. Factors Associated with Smoking', *International J. of Epidemiology*, Vol. 10 (3), 1981, pp. 223–31.

1981. The findings are useless as evidence that advertising induces children to smoke, but very useful as demonstrating illogic and the danger of making heroic conclusions. O'Connell *et al.* gathered data on teenage smoking, advertising recognition/approval, and the smoking habits of friends of teenage smokers. They found that teenagers who smoke are more likely to 'approve' of cigarette advertisements than those who do not smoke. This led them to the conclusion:

> 'that intervention in the field of cigarette advertising may be the most direct and effective means of reducing the prevalence of smoking in children.'

It would be difficult to find a statement which has less internal logic. Specifically, it is well known in marketing and confirmed by common sense that people who use the products advertised are more likely to approve of their advertisements than are non-users. Thus it is hardly surprising that teenagers who have chosen to smoke for other reasons, such as family or peer example, are more pre-disposed to approve of cigarette advertisements. It certainly does not demonstrate or even 'suggest' that advertising induces smoking. Indeed, the authors recognise at one point that it is difficult 'to identify which is the antecedent factor (approval of advertising or smoking behaviour)'. Moreover, even if 'approval of advertising' were the antecedent factor in the smoking decision, it would hardly imply, much less demonstrate, *causation.*

Finally, the authors assert that an earlier study conducted by them which found an overwhelming proportion of children who smoke claim to smoke only one brand, 'suggests to us that cigarette advertising plays a major role in encouraging children to commence and continue smoking'. This is a superb example of 'bootstrapping' a conclusion into an argument; and it illustrates the illogic which permeates much of the research by those who would ban tobacco advertising. The finding that advertising leads to brand loyalty tells us nothing whatsoever about the decision to begin or continue smoking.

The Alleged Effect of Advertising on Youth Brand Choice

Those who would ban tobacco advertising often argue that not only does advertising induce young people to smoke, but that further evidence of the pernicious effect of advertising is that adolescents tend to smoke most heavily advertised brands. It is again instructive to examine the evidence for this allegation.

(1) The Center for Disease Control (CDC) Study[38]

The 1993 study by the CDC is often cited for the proposition that advertising influences smoking behaviour of adolescents because it found that 86 per cent of US adolescents who purchased their own cigarettes purchased one of three brands. Several observations bear emphasis.

First, the 'adolescents' in the CDC study were aged 12-18 years, when 18-year-olds are entitled to vote in Federal elections.

Second, the CDC study is not about cigarette consumption and advertising, but about changes in brand preferences and advertising expenditures. It found that there was a connection between changes in advertising expenditures and changes in brand choice, though not a consistent correlation. For example, in both 1989 and 1993, the brands Marlboro, Camel and Newport were ranked first, second and third, respectively. Yet, between 1989 and 1993 brand preferences changed in the same direction as advertising expenditures for two of the brands, but moved in opposite directions for the third brand. Thus the CDC study does not even demonstrate a correlation between changes in brand preferences and changes in advertising expenditures. It most assuredly does not demonstrate that advertising expenditures caused changes in brand preferences. Moreover, given the data, it is impossible for the CDC or anyone else to know whether the changes in brand preference preceded or followed the changes in advertising expenditures since all data relate to 'stock' as opposed to 'flow' values.

---

[38] Center for Disease Control, 'Changes in the Cigarette Brand Preferences of Adolescent Smokers – United States, 1989–1993', *Morbidity and Mortality Weekly Reports*, Vol. 43 (32), 19 August 1994, pp. 577–81. (Hereinafter cited as MMWR.)

(2) The Goldstein Study[39]

Yet another study often put forward for the pernicious effect of advertising on smoking behaviour by youth is by Goldstein *et al.* in 1987. Indeed, this study has been held to prove (a) that young people smoke a smaller number of brands than adults as a consequence of advertising, and (b) that advertising leads to greater brand recognition and affects the decision to smoke.

Goldstein's study was based on a sample of 306 private high school students who were in the 9th through 12th grades. Using a slide presentation, Goldstein endeavoured to determine the extent and degree of brand and logo recognition. Among other things, he found that 'students who smoked more than one pack per week recognised nearly twice as many advertisements as students who were non-smokers'. This finding can certainly not be shown to support the hypothesis that advertising leads to more brand recognition among youth. The better interpretation is that smokers simply pay more attention to cigarette advertising as part of the brand selection process or are more likely to recognise their own brands.

(3) The Joe Camel Advertisements

One of the most widely known tobacco advertising campaigns is that by the R. J. Reynolds Tobacco Company which featured the company-created character, *Joe Camel*. It has been suggested that this advertising campaign has induced young people to smoke and that it illustrates the insidious effects of advertising by virtue of the fact that Joe Camel is well-recognised by American youth as well as adults.

That anti-tobacco advocates have held up Joe Camel as an illustration of the influence of advertising on youth is particularly interesting since the Federal Trade Commission (FTC), after a comprehensive review of the relevant studies and data, concluded that there is no relationship, that 'the evidence is not there'.

Yet another study of the effectiveness of the Joe Camel

---

[39] A. O. Goldstein *et al.*, 'Relationship between High School Student Smoking and Recognition of Cigarette Advertisements', *J. Paediatrics*, Vol. 110(3), March 1987, pp. 488–91.

campaign was by Fischer (1991),[40] who measured recognition of brand logos among almost 300 pre-school children aged 3–6 years. It found that 30 per cent of the 3-year-olds, and 90 per cent of the 6-year-olds correctly matched Joe Camel with a picture of a cigarette. To go on to argue that brand recognition induces smoking is spurious reasoning in the extreme.

The simple fact is that there is often a high degree of brand recognition among both adults and children who do not use a particular brand. Indeed, a 1995 study by Mizerski[41] demonstrates that children who recognised *Joe Camel* were more likely to dislike cigarettes. Further, while older children were more likely to recognise *Joe Camel*, they were actually less likely to like cigarettes. Indeed, at every age, children who recognised *Joe Camel* were more likely to dislike cigarettes than were children who did not recognise him. There is absolutely no evidence that Joe Camel imagery has led anyone to start smoking.

On the Effectiveness of 'Promotional' Advertising – the Advertising of Tobacco at Sporting Events

Anti-tobacco advocates often suggest that not only advertising should be banned, but also the use of trademarks and logos, such as Joe Camel on tee-shirts, baseball caps, etc. should be prohibited as well. It is further argued that sponsorship of sporting events by tobacco companies should also be forbidden. Such proposals presume of course that the use of logos converts the wearer into a 'walking billboard' and that such advertisements have an effect on children's disposition to start smoking.

(1) The Legality of Advertising/Trademark Restrictions

The first observation is that made by the Dean of the Law Faculty of Stockholm University, Ulf Bernitz, who said:

> 'General bans on logo licensing involving tobacco products would be incompatible with long-established principles of international

---

[40] P. M. Fischer *et al.*, 'Brand Logo Recognition by Children Aged 3 to 6 Years', *J. of the Am.. Med. Assn.*, Vol. 266, 1991, p. 3145 ff.

[41] R. Mizerski, 'The Relationship between Cartoon Trade Character Recognition and Attitude Toward Product Category in Young Children', *J. Marketing*, Vol. 59, 1995, pp. 58–70.

> trademark law.'[42]

To suppose that 'logo licensing' by tobacco companies is an attempt to increase cigarette consumption ignores the fact that the trademark/logo has value to the company as a separate product, and that by licensing its use the company can derive additional revenue. Thus, for example, Coca-Cola has licensed its trademark for use in connection with a line of clothing; Calvin Klein, Yves St Laurent, and Ralph Lauren have licensed their trademarks for use on products ranging from eyeglasses and underwear, to umbrellas and bedsheets. Similarly Dunhill, famous for pens, also makes cigarettes. To prevent a company using or licensing its trademarks would deprive the company of revenue. The expropriation would both violate international trademark law, and/or require the payment of compensation by the government.

Even if the legal argument were not sufficiently compelling, the argument that companies should be prohibited from utilising their brand names on non-tobacco paraphernalia or public events, is inherently illogical. It cannot be argued that tobacco companies sponsor events or license non-tobacco products, for the purpose of promoting increased consumption of tobacco in general. At most, it can be argued that tobacco company promotions are attempts to promote its own brand; that is, the advertising is brand specific, not generic. Thus, at most, it is designed to induce persons who already smoke to recognise and/or prefer the brand being advertised. It is inherently absurd to suggest that brand advertising is designed to promote consumption of other brands.

It must be emphasised again that there is no evidence that brand promotions have any effect on the disposition of young people to smoke. This was noted by the Legislative Council of the Parliament of Western Australia in 1990:

> 'Any decision to ban all forms of tobacco advertising, including sports sponsorship, is purely a political decision...not based on irrefutable empirical evidence.'[43]

---

[42] U. Bernitz, 'Logo Licensing of Tobacco Products – Can It be Prohibited?', *Eur. Intell. Prop. Rev.*, Vol. 4, 1990, pp. 137–39.

[43] Legislative Council, West. Australia Parliament, *Report of the Standing Comm. on Legis. in Relation to the Tobacco Bill*, 1990, p. 1.

(2) Slade's Work

One alleged study cited for the proposition that there is an association between various tobacco company promotional gifts and susceptibility to smoking turns out to be a series of slides presented to the 9th World Conference on Tobacco and Health in 1994 with absolutely no data or other information which would enable an independent researcher to assess their quality or the validity of the conclusions.[44]

(3) The 'Gray' Memorandum[45]

Yet another study often put forward as evidence that sponsorship, and so on, has an important impact on youth smoking is not a study at all but merely a two-page memorandum written by an anti-tobacco activist in Australia to members of the Australian Parliament in which he claims that sponsored events in certain Australian territories had a higher share of the youth smoking market than did non-sponsored events. Significantly, the study cited merely measures brand shares and makes no attempt to correlate it to sponsorship.

(4) Aitken's 1986 Study[46]

Perhaps the leading study which purports to demonstrate that sponsorship has an undesirable effect on youth smoking is the 1986 study by Aitken which alleges favourable associations between the sponsor's product and the event sponsored. This study of UK youth was designed to gauge the effect of various socio-demographic factors such as sex, age and socio-economic status, on awareness of cigarette sponsorships. It was not designed to gauge whether exposure to tobacco-sponsored events, or teams, engendered favourable feelings for tobacco products in the young people

---

[44] J. Slade *et al.*, 'Teenagers Participate in Tobacco Promotions', presented at the *9th World Conference on Tobacco and Health*, 10-14 October 1994.

[45] Memorandum from N. Gray, Director of the Anti-Cancer Council of Victoria, Australia, to all Members of the Federal Parliament of Australia, 15 December 1989.

[46] P.P. Aitken *et al.*, 'Children's Awareness of Cigarette Brand Sponsorship of Sports and Games in the UK', reported in *Health Educ. Res.*, Vol. 1(3), 1986, pp. 203–11.

surveyed. It is difficult to know why, then, this is so often invoked by anti-tobacco activists.

Embarrassingly for Aitken *et al.*, the authors found that 'few of the primary school children named Marlboro or John Player Special as being associated with motor-car racing'. Since this finding was clearly not what the authors wanted they attempted to get around it by asserting, with absolutely no supporting evidence, that 'this suggests that linkages or associations between brand names (or their visual cues) and exciting sports are often unconscious or, at the very least, not readily retrieved to consciousness'. Such an incredible example of 'bootstrapping' an hypothesis into a conclusion is unworthy of serious scholars and demonstrates the inherent bias of the authors.

(5) The Hoek Study[47]

An American study cited by the FDA is that of Hoek in 1993 which claimed promotions such as sports sponsorships 'affect those under age 18 by creating associations with events, teams or personalities with whom they identify' and thus have 'the potential to increase the rate at which young males smoke by negating the ill-effects associated with smoking'.

This 'research' was based on two groups of 100 young boys who were each shown a 15-minute video. The video seen by one group contained an advertisement promoting a tobacco company's sponsorship of a sporting event; the second group did not see this advertisement. It is difficult to know precisely what the authors were attempting to demonstrate by this 'test' since at most it could demonstrate the effect of a particular advertisement on the two groups; it could hardly demonstrate the effects of sponsorship on consumption or on predisposition to smoke.

The authors of this highly flawed study seem aware of its failings since they note that: 'non-smokers' general attitudes to smoking were not significantly affected by exposure to the sponsorship advertisement'. Moreover, Hoek *et al.* note that among the group of smokers in their test group the exposure to sponsorship

---

[47] E. G. Hoek *et al.*, 'Some Effects of Tobacco Sponsorship Advertisements on Young Males', *International J. of Advertising*, Vol. 12, 1993, pp. 8–34.

advertisement did not affect the smokers' brand choices.

Rather obviously, this led the authors to conclude that 'these findings do not, in themselves, constitute a case for legislation'. That they are cited in support of sponsorship bans suggests a lack of better evidence.

(6) Charlton et al. [48]

Appearing in 1997, after the FDA report, was a study by Charlton *et al.* reporting on their study of smoking behaviour by adolescents in 22 schools in England. The purpose of this study was to determine 'whether there is evidence that motor racing is associated with increased risk of smoking in children', 'whether regular smoking increases in association with watching motor racing', and 'whether watching motor racing has a significant effect when other known influences are taken into account'. Charlton *et al.* report the results for only 1,063 boys aged 12–14 who completed two questionnaires in the years 1994 and 1995.

The authors report that in the two years, 128, or 12 per cent, and 143, or 13.5 per cent, respectively, of the total boys reported that motor racing was their favourite sport and were more likely to 'name' Marlboro and Camel in the earlier year, 1994. No results are given for the year 1995. Moreover, it is unclear what is meant by the ability of the boys who liked motor racing to 'name' Marlboro and Camel. If, as the authors would seemingly suggest, the boys who watch motor racing are more readily able to recognise the Marlboro and Camel adverts and/or logos than those who do not watch motor racing, then these are hardly surprising results. As we have noted, the ability to identify a brand is radically different from a pre-disposition to consume it. Moreover, in view of the 1996 findings of Mizerski that children who recognised *Joe Camel* are also those who are more likely to dislike cigarettes, and that older children were more likely to recognise *Joe Camel* but less likely to like cigarettes, it is difficult to place much credence in Charlton *et al.*'s rather heroic conclusion that a ban on tobacco advertising would significantly decrease the smoking rate of young

---

[48] Anne Charlton, David White, and Sheila Kelly, 'Boys' Smoking and Cigarette-Brand-Sponsored Motor Racing', 350 *The Lancet*, 15 November 1997, p. 1474.

males. Indeed, Mizerski's findings could be interpreted to suggest precisely the opposite.

This study was regrettably endorsed by *The Lancet* as evidence in support of a ban on tobacco sponsorship of motor racing. This is most surprising for several reasons. *First*, it is difficult to understand why a scholarly journal would do anything other than present findings, not comment on them. *Second*, it is difficult to understand why an ostensibly scholarly journal would use the journalistic phrase of 'an opportunity to deliver the tobacco industry an important blow'. *Finally*, if a professional journal chooses to comment on published findings, its reputation would be enhanced if it subjected the findings to careful scrutiny, or some minimal standards of logic, before endorsing them.

Charlton *et al.*'s conclusions are not borne out by their reported work. For example, as Sadler[49] has pointed out, Charlton's conclusion that boys who like motor racing are more likely to smoke, with the implication that observation of tobacco advertisements induces them to smoke, relies on the fact that of the 1,063 boys who answered the Charlton questionnaire, only 125 seemingly liked motor racing, and of these only 16 started smoking. As Sadler notes:

> 'This base is so small that if only one boy had answered either question differently, the results would have lost their statistical significance – which is hardly a strong base on which to demand severe changes in public policy.'

Moreover, as Luik noted in a letter to *The Lancet*,[50] 'a study, such as Charlton's, which fails to control for the multiple risk factors for adolescent smoking, can tell us nothing about the causes of any adolescent's beginning to smoke'. Accordingly,

> 'a study of this type can in principle tell us only about the association of certain alleged predictors and adolescent smoking; it can never legitimately use the language of cause and effect nor provide evidence of causality.'

---

[49] P. A. Sadler, 'Letter to the Editor of Lancet', *The Lancet*, Vol. 351, 7 February 1998, p. 451.

[50] J. C. Luik, 'Letter to the Editor of *The Lancet*', *ibid.*, p. 452.

Luik further reminds *The Lancet*'s readers of Smee's correct observation that:

> 'awareness of advertising is at most a necessary condition for coming under its influence. It is not reliable evidence that advertising increases consumption.'

and that Smee had further correctly noted that 'it is also possible that those children who react most positively to advertising are already disposed to smoke'.

In other words, Smee recognised – as we have argued – that perception is not consumption.

The only conclusion which can properly be drawn from Charlton *et al.* is that while tobacco advertising *may be* associated with tobacco consumption, it does not follow that tobacco advertising induces people, particularly youngsters, to smoke. To move from observing an association to assuming causality is something which Smee warned about and which Charlton *et al.* chose to ignore. Such a leap of logic in the pages of an ostensibly scholarly journal – aimed at supporting an unprecedented denial of free speech – surely suggests a strong antipathy to smokers or tobacco companies at the outset.

7. *The State of Law Regarding Advertising of Tobacco Products in The European Community*

(1) Introduction

ON 6 JULY 1998, THE EUROPEAN PARLIAMENT and European Council published its Directive 98/43/EC which would substantially ban all advertising of any products containing tobacco in all member nations of the European Community, end sponsorship by tobacco companies of sporting events by 2006, end the free distribution of tobacco products, and largely prohibit the use of brand names by tobacco companies on non-tobacco products offered for sale within the EU. If implemented, the effects on the Community's tobacco industry, its advertising industry, and on tobacco consumers would be far-reaching. What is perhaps less obvious is that a strong precedent would have been established which could effectively remove any powers of member nations to prohibit any act which the EU apparatchiks might pass.

This section examines the legislative history of the Directive, its ostensible and actual purposes, and its likely legality under EU law. We conclude by noting some analogies with the expansion of US federal power *vis-à-vis* the States, via the 'commerce clause', in America.

(2) The Legislative History of the Directive

An early fore-runner of the present Directive was a proposal submitted to the European Commission in 1989 providing for a ban on advertising of tobacco products in publications which were intended for persons under 18.[1] There was no prohibition on advertising in the general press or on posters, and publications which complied with the proposed directive were to be given free circulation within the internal market. The legal basis for the Directive was Article 100a of the Treaty which established the

[1] OJ 1989 C 124/5, Com (89), 163 final 2.

European Community, giving the Community power to harmonise laws and regulations so as to promote free trade and the internal market of the Community.

In 1991 and 1992,[2] further drafts of the 1989 proposal were put forward under the same Article 100a with the same limited purpose of harmonising laws and regulations on commerce in tobacco products to advance the internal market. These drafts would have established a general ban on all forms of advertising, both direct and indirect, would have applied to non-tobacco products which employed similar brand names and/or trademarks, and would have prohibited free distribution of tobacco products. The proposed ban would have prohibited tobacco advertising within tobacco shops, if the advertising were visible from outside the premises. Finally, the 1991/92 directives would explicitly enable member states to introduce measures on advertising of tobacco products which they thought 'necessary to guarantee health'.

In December 1993, the EU Council's Legal Service ruled that the proposed 1991/92 Directive was unlawful. The basis of this opinion was that Article 100a was insufficient to justify such sweeping directives. The Legal Service concluded that:

- there was no real relationship between banning free distribution of tobacco products, and elimination of barriers to trade within the Community;
- even if it were thought that the advertising ban served to promote trade by harmonising laws on advertising, the virtual total ban was excessive and violated the principle of proportionality[3] since less restrictive means could readily be employed to achieve the ostensibly desired purpose; and
- that other provisions of the Treaty could not be employed as the basis for the proposed Directive.

In 1995, the Directorate-General for Research of the European

---

[2] For the 1991 Proposal, see OJ No. C 167, 26.6.1991, p. 3, and for the 1992 proposal see OJ No. C 129, 21.5.1992, p. 5.

[3] Simply put, the principle of proportionality requires that one cannot use a baseball bat or shotgun to kill a fly, but can employ only those means reasonably calculated to achieve the permissible results, e.g. a fly swatter.

Parliament commissioned research on the 'Division of Competencies in the EU'.[4] This work, carried out by Prof. J.H.H. Weiler and Franz Mayer, employed the proposed advertising bans of 1991/92 as vehicles to explore the extent of the powers of the EU in relation to those of its member nations. While the proposed EU ban was not the focal point, it was taken as a useful vehicle to explore the 'outer limits' or boundaries of the powers of the EU, and the likelihood that such legislation could serve to lessen the powers of the member states *vis-à-vis* the centre, and thus slowly but irrevocably break down carefully constructed constitutional constraints erected to ensure the European Community remained a *federal* community of delegated powers. Using the proposed tobacco ban as a 'case study', Weiler concluded that the Draft Directive was outside the Community's competence – that is, was *ultra vires*.

In September 1997 (after the election of the Blair Government), at a meeting of the EU Council, the Luxembourg presidency tabled a proposal purporting to contain the 'preliminary elements for a compromise'.[5] This proposal was not dramatically different from those of 1991/92, but included restrictions on sponsorship of sporting events, and eased the proposed advertising ban in publications published and printed in third countries, as well as in trade journals. These proposals were discussed in December 1997 at a meeting of the Council of Health Ministers, and in February 1998, were adopted as a 'Common Position'. In May 1998, the Legal Affairs Committee declared its opinion that the Common Position was illegal, despite adding new legal bases, Treaty articles 57(2) and 66, to the original Article 100a. Despite this rejection of the constitutionality of the proposed Directive, in June 1998 the EU Parliament approved the 'Common Position' which was published in the Official Journal on 7 July 1998 *ceteris paribus*, to go into effect two months thereafter.

---

[4] European Parliament, Directorate-General for Research, Political and Institutional Affairs Division, 'The Division of Competencies in the European Union', Political Series W-26 (Working Paper, March 1997). [Hereinafter cited as *Weiler*.]

[5] Council Document SN 3381/97.

(3) Legality of the Directive on Tobacco Advertising

(A) Jurisdiction of the Community

The European Community is a totally artificial community, in that its very existence is defined by the treaties which brought it into existence. Unlike nation-states, the Community has no original jurisdiction over any matter, but only the jurisdiction and powers which derive from the treaties creating it. Legislative powers which member states have not assigned to the Community stay with the member states. The European Court of Justice has said most clearly that the Community's powers cannot be described generally, but result from Treaty provisions vesting in the Community the particular power over a specified area of competency.[6]

It is important to note that the Community enjoys no competency in matters of public health. These matters are reserved for the member states. Title X of Article 129, introduced by the Maastricht Treaty, *encourages* the Community to co-operate in promoting public health, only in the form of research and the dissemination of health information and education. Article 129 expressly *excludes* 'any harmonisation of the laws and regulations of the Member States'.

As the authority on advertising law, Professor W. Skouris of the Faculty of Law of the Greek Aristotle University has said:

> 'a measure such as the proposed ban of advertising of tobacco products – if we accept that it primarily or mainly seeks to serve public health – cannot be imposed by the European Community through the harmonisation method.'

The professor elaborated that before Article 129, harmonisation on public health was not totally prohibited and could, at least, have been achieved through the procedure of the EC Treaty Article 235. After the Maastricht Treaty this option has been ruled out.[7]

Thus prohibition of harmonisation in the public health policy

---

[6] See Weiler, *op. cit.*, and especially pp. 27–29.

[7] W. Skouris, 'Legal Opinion on the Proposed Directive on the Total Ban of the Advertising of Tobacco Products', in T. Stein (ed.), *The Proposed Directive Banning Tobacco Advertising and Sponsorship: Why there is No Legal Basis*, Brussels: Confederation of European Community Cigarette Manufacturers Ltd., 1998, p. 69. [Hereinafter cited as *CECCM*.]

area by member states could not be more clear.

It should be added, as a matter of logic and of EU case law,[8] that the Community does enjoy the power to affect areas which might otherwise be denied to it, provided this is *merely an ancillary and incidental effect* of the exercise of powers which do lie within the competence of the Community. This merely reflects a recognition that most laws have some tangential effect on areas beyond the immediate purpose of the law itself. However, under general constitutional principles, such laws will enjoy judicial approval if and only if the secondary effects are merely incidental and ancillary. If these effects are substantial, then the law cannot be permitted to stand.

When considering the jurisdiction of the Community, it should constantly be borne in mind that the principal purposes for which the Community was created were to promote increased trade, competition and economic well-being, within the member states of the Community. Its very *raison d'être* is 'the approximation of the laws of Member states to *the extent required for the proper functioning of the common market*'. [9] This is the very polestar of the Community's existence.

(B) The Legality of Tobacco Advertising Directive

(i) Legal Bases of the Directive

We have seen that the legal basis for the original advertising ban was Article 100a. However, the present ban proposal adds, as legal bases, Articles 57(2) and 66, presumably because of the demonstration of Weiler and others that Article 100a was an inadequate platform. Lest it be thought that reference to legal bases is grounded in a mere legalistic exercise, it should be recalled that the Community enjoys only those powers expressly delegated to it, and all powers not so delegated are reserved to the member states. Moreover, Article 190 requires that the legal bases shall be expressly stated. Specifically, this Article says:

---

[8] Cf. Case C-271/94, *Parliament v. Council* [1996] ECR I – 1689, as well as the Court's opinion in Case C-84/94, *United Kingdom v. Council* [1996] ECR I – 5755, in which the Court suggests that the Applicant would have prevailed had it been able to demonstrate that the harm complained of was more than an incidental effect of the EU's legislation.

[9] As cited in Weiler, *op. cit.*, p. 27.

'Regulations, directives and decisions adopted jointly by the European Parliament and the Council [as is the tobacco advertising ban], and such acts adopted by the Council or the Commission, shall state the reasons on which they are based and shall refer to any proposal or opinion which was required to be obtained pursuant to this Treaty.'

It was accordingly incumbent on the Parliament and Council to state expressly the legal bases on which the directive was issued. And, since Articles 57(2) and 66 were later added, it is not unreasonable to deduce that Parliament and Council were persuaded that Article 100a was insufficient.

(ii) The Directive's Preamble

Moreover, the present directive sought to circumvent the prohibition on public health legislation by claiming in the preamble that the purpose of the Directive was to harmonise laws, regulations, and administrative provisions on advertising and sponsorship which would otherwise create barriers to trade in the media for advertising and sponsorship, thereby distorting competition and impeding the internal market.

Courts do not generally pay undue attention to the alleged reasons parliamentarians advance for the laws and regulations they enact. As the ECJ said in the landmark Titanium Dioxide case in 1991:

'In the context of the organisation of the powers of the Community, the choice of legal basis for a measure *may not depend simply on an institution's conviction as to the objective pursued*, but must be based on objective factors which are amenable to judicial review...*Those factors include in particular the aim and content of the measures.*'[10]

Moreover, the Court is not so foolish as to be persuaded that the intent of parliament is that described in the Preamble. It is a common 'rule of statutory interpretation' for virtually all jurisdictions that the preamble to legislation, while sometimes helpful in discerning the intent of the legislature, is often little more than 'boilerplate' – signifying little or nothing. Nevertheless, according to one commentator: 'All these questions involve so

---

[10] Case C300/90, *Commission v. Council (Titanium Dioxide)* [1991] ECR 1-2867, para. 10. This is the Court's standard formula regarding the legal basis for legislation.

many imponderables that it will almost always be possible for the Court, if it wishes, to find grounds for upholding the measure.'[11]

However, this does not mean the Court is unconstrained. Quite the contrary: in a case brought by the United Kingdom against the Council, on the grounds that the measures regarding harmonising of hours of work under Article 118A were improperly grounded, and should have been based on Articles 100 and 235 which require unanimity by the Council, rather than a qualified majority, the Court said the UK would have prevailed if it had been able to establish that the directive was adopted with the exclusive or main purpose of achieving an end other than that on which the directive was grounded. In which case the Court would have found for the UK and against the Directive.[12]

The conclusion, then, must be that the mere language of the preamble of the present directive will not suffice to save it. The Courts should look at substance.

Returning to the directive to ban tobacco advertising, it cannot be reasonably argued that its real purpose is to eradicate barriers to trade in media services, as is its ostensible purpose. Nor can it reasonably be argued that its purpose is to expand trade in tobacco products. Rather, a fair reading of the directive is that it intends to ban the advertising so as to promote public health – which we have seen is not permitted under the Treaty.

(iii) The Directive

It is instructive to examine the directive to see what, in fact, it mandates.

(a) Article 1 re-iterates the 'boilerplate' purpose to 'approximate' the laws, regulations and administrative provisions of the member states relating to the advertising and sponsorship of tobacco products. This is rather different from the Preamble which states the purpose was to ensure that the laws, regulations, and administrative provisions of the member states regarding the 'products which serve as the media for such adver-

---

[11] Nicolas Emiliou, 'Opening Pandora's Box: The Legal Basis for Community Measures Before the Court of Justice', *European Law Review*, 1994, p. 488.

[12] Case C-84/94, *United Kingdom v. Council* [1996] ECR I-5755, 1c, para. 70.

tising...and...services in this area' are 'approximated', as mentioned in Preamble section (1). That section of the Preamble refers to harmonising differences in media and media services, while the purpose stated in Article 1 is to harmonise the laws, etc. regarding advertising and sponsorship of tobacco products themselves. Thus reference to harmonising alleged differences in media services and the vehicles for media transmission has been abandoned as we move from the Preamble to the first Article of the Directive. This is not a mere 'legalism' since the Community, in publishing the directive, has argued that the damage to free trade in the internal market occurs from the use of different media and media services. On the face of the Directive, it does not assert that the Community has the competence to regulate advertising *per se*; nor has it argued that advertising, *per se*, gives rise to trade barriers. The alleged concern of the Community is divergences in media services and products – not the media or messages themselves. To argue that the Community has the power to regulate the message itself would clearly cause it to violate fundamental rights of Community citizens which have been held by ECJ case law to be an integral component of Community law.[13] We shall return to this issue, but suffice it for now to observe that the alleged reason for 'approximating' the laws is to ensure that differences in advertising media services do not impede trade within the internal market.

Whether differences in media services and products are so substantial as to impede trade within the Community is an empirical matter. There is no showing in the directive, or its legislative history, that any differences in advertising of tobacco products, or the media in which tobacco is advertised, are so substantial as to interfere with free trade in either tobacco products, or the media in which they are advertised. Indeed, John Meade, of Arthur Cox, Solicitors, Dublin, and a former Lecturer in EC Law at Queen's University, Belfast, has noted that '...less than five percent of EC print media sales are exported between the Member

[13] See, for example, Case 29/69, *Stauder* [1969] ECR 419 (425), para. 7; case 11/70, *Internationale Handelsgesellschaft* [1970] ECR 1125 (1135), para.3; Case 4/73, *Nold* [1974] ECR 491 (507), para. 13; Case 44/79, *Hauer* [1979] ECR 3727 (3744), paras. 13 *et seq*.

States'.[14] Similarly, Prof. Weiler has noted that, by definition, stationary advertising (billboards, posters) are not media which have a trans-frontier market. [15] Weiler has similarly noted that, as regards advertising in newspapers and magazines, '...local advertising "newspapers" have no market whatsoever beyond their locality and certainly no conceivable European market'.[16]

Similarly, 'advertising inserts' in printed media are, Weiler notes, almost invariably local in nature. International or European editions of the newspapers do not carry the marketing inserts, which add to costs of transportation. Moreover, if, in fact, the real goal of the Community were to eliminate barriers to trade in newspapers and other print media then the simple expedient of preventing such inserts in print media distributed outside national borders would suffice. According to Weiler, the simple fact is that:

> 'of the total number of newspaper and magazine titles, only a very small fraction has any actual and potential intra-Community trade effect.'

(b) Article 2 defines advertising as 'any form of commercial communication with the aim of the direct or indirect effect of promoting a tobacco product'. Communications between professionals in the tobacco trade are exempted.

The inclusion of sponsorship in this definition of advertising provides yet further indication that the real goal is to eliminate tobacco advertising, not to co-ordinate media services and promote the internal market. The various sporting, cultural, and similar events, are local in nature. Certainly, nationals of one country might attend an event sponsored by a tobacco company in another country, but this argument would logically permit the EU to regulate virtually any commercial activity, if not any aspects of EU citizens' lives, since they might find themselves in another country. Moreover, while sponsored events are frequently shown on television which does cross national borders, there are less restrictive methods to ensure that the advertising is not observed in

---

[14] John Meade, 'Legal Basis for Proposed Directive on Tobacco Advertising and Sponsorship', in CECCM, *op. cit.*, p. 86.

[15] Weiler, *op. cit.*, p. 41.

[16] Weiler, *op. cit.*, p. 40.

those countries where it is prohibited.

Article 2 also prohibits the use of brand names, trademarks, and other distinctive features of tobacco products which do not mention tobacco. This is, arguably, a 'taking of the intellectual property' of tobacco companies, without compensation, in violation of the World Trade Organisation rules, despite Section 7 of the Preamble which commits the EU to upholding its 'obligations at the international level'.

(c) Article 3(1) clearly and unambiguously states that 'all forms of advertising and sponsorship shall be banned in the Community'. Article 3(2) attempts to cure the problem of the use of intellectual property by permitting tobacco companies to use their trademarks provided they do not promote tobacco products, and provided the trademark or brand name was used for the non-tobacco product prior to the introduction of the directive. Moreover, the trademark or brand name must be used in a manner which is distinctively different from its use with the tobacco product.

To the extent that brand names enable foreign competitors more readily to enter national markets by capitalising on their well-known name, they are more readily able to sell their goods. This is as true for tobacco products as for fountain pens, handbags, and perfumes – all of which are sold by companies which also sell tobacco goods. Clearly, by prohibiting companies from making use of their well-known brand names to penetrate a market dominated by a locally well-known national tobacco company, the EU directive will tend to increase the quasi-monopolistic position of a national manufacturer, and retard competition in the internal market. It is not necessary to be a highly trained economist to realise that preventing Dunhill employing its good name in France or Germany will tend to entrench the position of French, or German, tobacco manufacturers and vendors. It will certainly not tend to increase trade or competition in the internal market.

(d) Article 3 (4) prohibits the distribution of free samples of tobacco products. Like the blanket prohibition on print advertising (including stationary advertising), it makes clear that the purpose is not to promote the internal market, as required under Article 100a. Since distribution typically takes place by promoters handing samples to individuals, the activity is purely local in nature and has no effect on the trans-national market. The counter-argument that recipients of free samples might subsequently purchase the product, and thus affect trade in the Community is, *firstly*, speculative, since recipients are likely to be nationals who later purchase the good within their own nations, and *secondly*, a clear admission that such activity will tend to enhance, not limit, the internal market. Moreover, as already noted, to the extent that giving free samples enables 'outsiders' to pierce a market dominated by a national company, competition, and the internal market, are thereby enhanced.

It is worth noting that the ban on free distribution of tobacco products was one of the substantive grounds on which the Legal Service earlier said that the 1992 version of the present directive was *ultra vires,* being incorrectly based on Article 100a. It is difficult to see why this earlier opinion should be revised since this prohibition can hardly avoid detracting from the internal market.

(e) Article 3(5) eliminates from the ban communications between people in the tobacco trade which are exempted from the Article's definition of advertising; exempts the display of tobacco products and prices at sales outlets; permits advertising in stores, and in their shop-fronts, and, finally, exempts publications carrying advertisements from third countries entering the EU, provided they are not principally intended for the EU market.

It is difficult to understand why publications are caught in the net of this provision since they are mostly designed to be read in a single country and those publications of a given country, which are designed to be sold in another country, can be and are readily modified for foreign readers. This would meet the directive's alleged desire to prevent differences in advertising creating trade barriers, and thus distorting competition in publications which move between member states.

A second observation on Article 3(5) is that, presumably, advertising in stores and store fronts visible to the passing public is not prohibited. This is particularly interesting in view of the earlier argument put forward for the regulation of posters that 'people in one Member State are increasingly coming into contact with the other Member States' media, including posters'.[17] Weiler has mocked the suggestion that the EU could regulate stationary posters merely because visitors from another member state may observe them as an absurdity since

> 'if this were so, the Community would have unlimited competence to legislate in every single social field in which there is a chance for a citizen of one Member state to come into contact with the social regimes of another.' [18]

(f) Article 4 is especially interesting for economists, as giving rise to the possibility of 'rent seeking' by anti-tobacco groups. Thus it provides that member states shall adopt national measures which ensure adequate means of monitoring and enforcing the directive. It expressly includes provisions whereby

> 'persons or organisations with a legitimate interest under national law in the withdrawal of advertising which is incompatible with this directive may take legal proceedings against such advertising or bring such advertising to the attention of an administrative body competent to give a ruling on complaints to institute the appropriate legal proceedings.'

Such language gives rise to the possibility of private enforcement of the directive including the possibility that anti-tobacco groups may engage in 'rent seeking'. It strongly encourages member states to permit a private cause of action, even if this may violate judicial norms and practice in the jurisdiction.

(g) Given repeated statements that the ostensible purpose of the Directive is to harmonise laws, rules and regulations regarding trade in media and media services, Article 5 is especially illuminating. It expressly permits

> 'member states laying down, in accordance with the Treaty, such stricter requirements concerning the advertising or sponsorship of tobacco products as they deem necessary to guarantee the health protection of individuals.'

---

[17] *Explanatory Memorandum of the Commission Doc. 0437EN91800*, 'Basis of Community Action', 8 March 1991, as cited in Weiler, *op. cit.*, p. 38.

[18] Weiler, *ibid.*, p. 39.

Put differently, this article invites member nations to pass legislation which is at variance with that of other member nations – despite the ostensible purpose being to harmonise trade in media services. The reason is that health is a matter which the treaties creating the EU expressly leave to member states. Thus this Article implicitly acknowledges that the EU has no competence over member states regarding health issues. In so doing the article must allow that if member states deem less restrictive measures to be appropriate for the health of their citizens, they are logically at liberty to ignore the EU directive, and introduce less restrictive measures. A fair reading of the language of this Article must therefore lead to the conclusion that the directive is designed to promote public health – a matter clearly beyond the competency of the Community.

(iv) The Constitutionality of the Directive under National Law

Taken as a whole, the Directive is likely to place the EU on a collision course with the governments of Austria, Denmark and Germany, among others. The Austrian Constitutional Court has, in repeated rulings, held that a comprehensive, absolute ban on advertising violates the Austrian constitution. In other words, the Constitutional Court has held that commercial advertising enjoys constitutional protection, and is guaranteed by the European Commission of Human Rights (ECHR) Article 10.[19] Further, the Court has held that

> 'Article 10 does not aim at certain forms of expression; it rather intends to guarantee open processes of communication in all sectors of society…Thus, the Court concurs with the ECHR…in that commercial advertising falls into the realm of the protection of Article 10 paragraph 1, too.' [20]

---

[19] *Frowein-Peukert (EMRK - Kommentar,* 2d ed., 1996, p. 389), citing *markt intern* (EuGRZ 1996, 3021) noted that 'in the case of market intern the Court, (i.e. the ECHR) clearly confirmed that information of a commercial nature falls into the scope of Article 10'. (Cited in B. Raschauer, 'Legal Opinion Concerning the…Proposed EC Directive Relating to the Advertising and Sponsorship of Tobacco Products into National Law Under Austrian Constitutional Law', in T. Stein (ed.), *The Proposed Directive Banning Tobacco Advertising and Sponsorship, op. cit.*, p. 17.)

[20] VfSlg 10948/1986 as cited in Raschauer, *ibid.*, p. 17.

As Rauschauer has noted, the Austrian Constitutional Court:

> 'would be obliged to void such legislation, as in any other case the Republic of Austria would be threatened by a condemnation by the European Court of Human Rights.'

A potential constitutional crisis for the Community does not originate solely from Austria. The Courts of Denmark and Germany, among others, are likely to find the directive invalid under their laws, and prohibit national officials from enforcing it. Professor of European Law at the University of Copenhagen, Dr H. Rasmussen, has predicted that 'grave consequences may follow especially if the [European] Court does not invalidate the...act on the ground that it is *ultra vires*'.[21] He further noted:

> 'The German Constitutional Court as well as the Danish Supreme Court, both ruling on challenges of the constitutionality of, respectively, the German and Danish acts of Ratification of the Maastricht Treaty, threatened to disapply a Community enactment if it is based on an interpretation of an article empowering the Community to act which the national court deems to make the act *ultra vires*.'

The German courts are particularly protective of the rights of citizens under the Basic Law and are quite likely to find that the directive violates Article 5 of the Basic Law which protects Freedom of Expression, of Information, of the Press, and of Art. In addition, the Directive arguably violates the Basic Law by virtue of violating Article 12, which protects freedom of professional activity; and Article 14, which protects the right to property.

The fundamental freedoms of expression and the rest protected under Article 5 are subject to limitation by general statutes. However, as Rabe as noted,[22] general statutes

> 'are not directed against a specific opinion or against the process of free opinion-forming and the freedom of information as such, but which serve to protect a legal interest which is absolutely entitled to protection, without reference to any specific information or opinion.'

---

[21] H. Rasmussen, 'Legal Opinion on the Question of Whether there is a Legal Basis in the Community Treaty Warranting the Adoption of the Amended Draft Directive Concerning the Harmonisation of Legislative, Statutory and Administrative Provisions of Member States as Regards Advertising of Tobacco Products', CECCM, *op. cit.*, p. 29.

[22] Rabe, *op. cit.*, p. 50.

Since the directive is directed against tobacco advertising, specifically, it is difficult to see how a court could conclude this is a *general statute*. Similarly, as its clear purpose is against those who advocate smoking, it is plainly directed against 'a specific opinion' and 'against the process of free opinion-forming...' Again, it is difficult to see how German courts could uphold it.

Paragraph 1 of Article 5 of the Basic Law protects freedom of the press, including broadcasting, under German case law, and has been extended even to the advertising sections of newspapers and magazines.[23] A total advertising ban infringes on this basic freedom.

Finally, it should be noted that the Basic Law provides for the right to property, which German courts have held to include trademarks.[24] As already noted, the ban would deprive the owners of trademarks of the right to use their property. A restriction which is disproportionate to the alleged objective of harmonising competition, which impinges on the very essence of property rights, and which could serve to endanger a company's existence, is unlikely to be upheld by the Courts.

(C) Reasons for Including Articles 57(2) and 66

As we have seen, the present Directive is no longer based solely on Article 100a, but also on the additional legal bases of Articles 57(2) and 66(10). At first reading, this is rather curious, since Article 57(2) refers to the right of establishment, and gives the European Parliament and the Council power to

> 'issue directives for the co-ordination of the provisions laid down by the law, regulation or administrative action of Member States concerning the taking up and pursuit of activities as self-employed persons.'

Similarly, Article 66(1) advances the scope of Article 57(2) to the free provision of services. The ostensible reason for including these articles as legal bases is given in paragraph 1 of the directive which asserts that differences in legislation in the member states are 'likely to give rise to barriers...to freedom to provide services in

---

[23] BVerfGE 21, 271 (278); 64, 108 (114).

[24] BVerfGE 51, 193 (217).

this area [of advertising or sponsorship of tobacco products]'.

It is difficult to understand how a total ban on advertising and sponsorship of tobacco products could possibly further self-employment in the provision of media services, or the free provision of such services. Indeed, the directive would totally eliminate the provision of such services. It is not unreasonable, then, to hypothesise that the real reason for inclusion of these articles as legal bases for the directive is quite different from this ostensible one.

It is also not unreasonable to suggest that the drafters of the revised Directive, acting out of caution, included Articles 57(2) and 66(1) because they were part of the base on which directive 89/552, providing for a total ban on television advertising, rests. Television advertising was prohibited. This directive has withstood legal challenge for two principal reasons.

In the *first* place, television, by its very nature trancends national borders and, to the extent legislation in the several nations differs, the ability of vendors to sell their wares is affected. Thus if a seller is located in a nation which has very restrictive laws about what may be advertised on television, it may be at a competitive disadvantage compared with a seller of similar products domiciled in a less restrictive régime. Thus, harmonising laws on advertising may be argued to promote the internal market.

In the *second* place, its clear and dominant aim was to promote the free broadcasting of television programmes throughout the Community. Articles 10 to 21 enunciate minimum rules and standards on television advertising. Thus, arguably its dominant purpose was to ensure that differences in such regulations did not jeopardise the free circulation of television programmes.

While we would argue that the total ban on TV advertising of tobacco products remains disproportionate, it is also difficult to disagree with Professor Caporoti (a former judge of the European Court of Justice, and now a professor of European Law at Rome University) and Professor Daniele (of European Law at Trieste University) who have observed that:

> 'Obviously, the ban provided for by Article 13 could not be regarded in itself as a measure aiming at the elimination of barriers to the provision of services in the field of televised advertising for tobacco products. However, viewed in the context of the Directive, the ban

represented a minor element, which was clearly instrumental to attainment of the main aim of the measure. Its inclusion in a directive based on Articles 57.2 and 66 could therefore be "tolerated". In contrast, the total ban on advertising and sponsorship for tobacco products provided for by the draft Directive [98/43/EC], far from being a minor element in the context of a measure aiming at the elimination of barriers to the provision of a particular type of services, represents the key element, the very core of the entire measure.'[25]

Clearly, what the drafters of the present Directive wished to do was to 'lever' the legal bases of the total ban on television advertising into a total ban on advertising and sponsorship in order to increase its chances of judicial acceptance. Caporoti and Daniele exercised immense restraint when they concluded:

'A total ban on the provision of a specific service which had been previously allowed can in no way be regarded as a measure falling within the scope of Articles 57.2 and 66.1.'

More bluntly, the very idea that somehow the internal market in the provision of media services or products advertised in such media will be enhanced by total abolition of advertising can only be characterised as an absurdity. Rather than promoting competition, an advertising ban will clearly entrench the market shares of established tobacco manufacturers and vendors in the several nations.

(4) Implications of the Directive for the Federal Principles of the European Union

(A) Introduction

The EU is a *federal* union; that is, it is not only an 'artificial' creature defined by the treaties which created it but, in assenting to the founding treaties, the member nations expressly assented to explicit restraints on their own sovereignty and power, as well as on the power of the Community. Federal states the world over are characterised by an express division of powers and competencies into four major categories:

- those powers which the constituent member states delegate

[25] CECCM, *op. cit.*, p. 97.

exclusively to the federal state;

- those powers which are expressly reserved to the several member states;

- those powers which may be concurrently exercised by the central state, and the constituent members; and, lastly,

- in some federal systems there are what Weiler has denoted 'frame' powers, that is, the authority of the central government to establish general policies and/or guidelines, with the specific powers to enact legislation in support of the centrally-dictated policies determined by the member states.

Enumerating the powers of the centre and the sub-units of government provides a seemingly clear separation of competencies between the two. This seeming certainty may, however, be misleading. One reason the apparent division of powers may be more apparent than real is that, as we have seen, virtually all governmental acts have effects which are tangential to their direct purpose. When this occurs, the judiciary is often called upon to define the limits, or relative powers, of the centre and the localities. The dangers which attach to judicial demarcation of central government competencies from those of the member governments in a federal system is well illustrated by experience of the US federal system to which we now briefly turn.

(B) The American Experience – Toward Increased Centralisation of Governmental Power

The underlying theoretical structure of the US Constitution is one of dual sovereignty. The USA was initially intended to be a union of sovereign states which combined to create yet another sovereign, the central or federal government. Each governmental unit was to be sovereign, and the Constitution enumerates those powers which are exclusively the domain of the central government. Moreover, by the 10th Amendment, which was passed virtually simultaneously at the time of the adoption of the Constitution, those powers which were not vested in the central government were expressly reserved for the several states, or the people in those states. It was thought that such explicit language would provide a 'bright line' which would enable legislators, the judiciary, and the executive of the several units of government to know, with clarity and certainty, their relative powers.

This illusion of dual sovereignty, and states' sovereignty, was shattered first by the American Civil War, and, more recently, by judicial decision in a series of cases which successfully served to assert central supremacy, and to convert the US from a federal system into a largely unitary one. The vehicle for this judicial revolution was the Commerce Clause of the Constitution[26] which empowered the US Congress to 'regulate commerce with foreign nations and among the several states, and with the Indian nations'.

The purpose of this clause was, not unlike the treaties forming the European Union, to ensure free trade among the several states, and to end the protectionist practices so prevalent among the states under the Articles of Confederacy. Not unlike the framers of the European Community, a principal architect of the US Constitution, James Madison, observed in 1787, in his 'Notes on the Confederacy', that

> 'the practice of many states in restricting the commercial intercourse with other States…is certainly adverse to the spirit of the Union, and tends to beget retaliating regulations, not less expensive and vexatious in themselves than they are destructive of the general harmony.'[27]

Simply put, the framers of the American federal system, not unlike the architects of the EU, wished to promote free trade within the community.

For much of its history, the Supreme Court, when called upon to determine whether particular federal laws passed under the Commerce Clause exceeded the power of the Congress and impinged on the powers of the States, required that the federal law regulated an act which had a direct effect on commerce. This meant that many federal laws were struck down as unconstitutional

---

[26] US Constitution, Article I, section 8, para. 3.

[27] James Madison, 'Notes on the Confederacy', April 1787, in *Letters and Writings of James Madison*, Vol. 1, pp. 1,769–1,793. Published by Order of Congress. Philadelphia: J.B. Lippincott and Co., 1865.

usurpations of state powers. In the 1930s, during the height of the 'New Deal', faced with F.D. Roosevelt's well-known threat to 'pack' the Supreme Court, the Court upheld Congress's power to regulate any activity, local or interstate, which – either in itself or in combination with other activities – had a 'substantial economic effect upon', or 'effect on movement in', interstate commerce.[28] This case was quickly followed by others in which the Court continually expanded the power of Congress to regulate a variety of activities, as long as *some* effect, however remote, on interstate commerce could be found or inferred. As but one example, in the classic case of *Wickard v. Filburn*,[29] the Court held that the Congress could control a farmer's production of wheat for home consumption on the grounds that it meant it was withdrawn from interstate commerce, which Congress had the right to regulate under Article I.

Similarly, in 1941, the Court upheld the right of the federal government to regulate wages and hours of production in the manufacture and sale of goods and federal controls over intrastate marketing and handling of goods, on the rationale that those who take advantage of interstate markets, as either buyers, sellers, or distributors of goods which are in, or affected by, interstate commerce can be subjected to whatever conditions the federal government wishes to impose, so long as they do not violate independent Constitutional rights.[30]

This extension of Congressional power to regulate commerce has extended so far that, since 1936, only twice has it been held that a federal law exceeded the powers of Congress to regulate interstate commerce. Today, it is difficult to think of any federal regulation or law affecting private behaviour which could not be found to be justified as a legitimate exercise of the commerce power, as defined by judicial ruling. The only limits on the reach of federal government on behaviour are provided by *other* provisions of the Constitution, for example, the Bill of Rights.

Not only has judicial interpretation of the commerce clause

---

[28] *NLRB v. Jones & Laughlin Steel Corp.*, 301 U.S. 1 (1937).

[29] *Wickard v. Filburn*, 317 U.S. 111 (1942).

[30] *United State v. Darby*, 289 U.S. 224 (1941).

served to alter the nature of the American polity from a largely federal to a largely unitary State, but the point has been reached where it may safely be said that there is federal supremacy over all local commercial activities unless otherwise permitted by Congress. Several judicial doctrines which have arisen in American jurisprudence, that bear on the EU Tobacco Advertising Directive, are the doctrines of (a) super-session and (b) pre-emption. The *first* holds that any otherwise valid act of the federal government supersedes any state or local action that conflicts with it, the only exception being where Congress explicitly encourages state regulation.

The *second* judicial doctrine which has emerged from American jurisprudence that bears on the EU Directive, and the relative powers of the centre and member states, is the pre-emption doctrine, which holds that where there is an otherwise valid federal statute or regulation governing an area of human activity, it may expressly or implicitly be said to usurp and 'occupy' the entire field thus regulated, so as to preclude even non-conflicting state or local regulation of the same general subject. This doctrine has proved highly destructive of state and local powers.

(C) Conclusions

The framers of the Treaties creating the European Union very carefully enumerated which powers were to be the sole competencies of the central government, and which were to be reserved to the member states. While, in principle, such enumeration is desirable, it overlooks the extent to which central government legislation and regulation necessarily has indirect, or tangential, effects which will clash with powers vested in member states. The present advertising directive is one example. While the ostensible purpose of the directive is to harmonise trade in media services, its real purpose is to regulate the sale and distribution of tobacco products on the grounds of health. The framers recognised that attempts directly to regulate the sale and distribution of tobacco products would be struck down by the European Court as clear intrusions into public health, which is expressly reserved for the member states. Accordingly, they determined to legislate in an area otherwise prohibited to them under the guise of regulating commerce.

The American experience shows how incremental extensions of the Commerce Clause have permitted the USA to be turned from a federal into a virtually unitary system, in which the States are little more than administrative units of central government. While proponents of anti-tobacco legislation may rejoice if this Directive passes judicial scrutiny, they would do well to contemplate the further forces of centralisation which must thereby be unleashed.

8. Conclusion Regarding the Influence of Advertising on the Consumption of Tobacco Products

IN VIEW OF THE LACK OF EVIDENCE THAT THE PROCLIVITY OF YOUNG PEOPLE TO SMOKE is affected by the sponsorship of sporting, cultural or related events, or by the use of tobacco company logos on articles of clothing, sports equipment, and so on, it is difficult to disagree with Richard Luers, President of the New York Metropolitan Museum of Art, who said of proposals to ban tobacco sponsorship of art programmes, that:

> 'Private sector support of the arts involves two basic freedoms of choice: the potential grantor may not wish to participate; the grantee may or may not wish to accept that which has been offered. These two freedoms serve to rationalise both the business and cultural interest in terms of the ultimate societal interest. They need not, in our opinion, be further curbed by unnecessarily restrictive legislation.'[1]

This is what proposed restrictions on tobacco and tobacco advertising endeavour to do: restrict individual freedom to choose and restrict freedom of information. Only those with a disdain for the rights of individuals and who wish to substitute decision-making by the 'Nanny, or Orwellian, State' for decisions by free and independent individuals would support such restrictions.

As we saw in Section 2, the law in the United Kingdom and other Anglo-jurisdictions requires the state to demonstrate not only that advertising gives rise to a permissible government interest, but that the means proposed to further that interest are both the least restrictive available and reasonably calculated to achieve the end. The burden of persuasion is especially heavy, since the state proposes restricting freedom of speech and of the press. Our review of the evidence on the alleged effects of tobacco advertising, at a minimum, demonstrates that it is not possible for the state to carry this burden in the absence of convincing evidence that tobacco

---

[1] 'Arts Program Publisher Hits Measures to Ban Tobacco Ads', *Washington Post*, 12 August 1987, p. F-7.

advertising either induces anyone, including the young, to begin smoking, or serves to increase the aggregate amount of tobacco consumed.

Even if there remained some shadow of doubt, a prohibition on advertising would be wholly disproportionate. It should furthermore be wholly unacceptable to all who cherish liberal values and decry the process by which individual freedoms have been progressively eroded by political expediency during the present century.

Corporate Governance:

Accountability in the Marketplace

Elaine Sternberg

1. Businesses and corporations are not the same thing: not all corporations are businesses, and most businesses are not corporations. Whereas 'business' designates a particular objective, 'corporation' designates a particular organisational structure.
2. Corporate governance refers to ways of ensuring that corporate actions, assets and agents are directed at achieving the corporate objectives established by the corporation's shareholders (as set out in the Memorandum of Association or comparable constitutional document).
3. Many criticisms of corporate governance are based on false assumptions about what constitutes ethical conduct by corporations, and confusions about what corporate governance is.
4. Protests against takeovers, 'short-termism', redundancies and high executive remuneration are typically objections to specific corporate outcomes, not criticisms of corporate governance.
5. Many misguided criticisms of the Anglo-Saxon model come from confusing corporate governance with government: it is a mistake to criticise corporations for not achieving public policy objectives, and for not giving their stakeholders the rights and privileges commonly associated with citizenship.
6. Some criticisms of the traditional Anglo-Saxon model of corporate governance are justified. There are serious practical obstacles that prevent shareholders from keeping their corporations and corporate agents properly accountable.
7. Though commonly praised, the German and Japanese systems are considerably less capable of achieving the definitive purpose of corporate governance than the Anglo-Saxon model is. Neither is designed to protect, nor typically used for protecting, property rights.
8. The increasingly popular stakeholder theory is also incapable of providing better corporate governance. Stakeholder theory is incompatible with all substantial objectives and undermines both private property and accountability.
9. Regulation that attempts to improve corporate governance by limiting shareholders' options, and reducing their freedom to control their own companies as they choose, is necessarily counterproductive.
10. The way to respond to flaws in current Anglo-Saxon corporate governance mechanisms is to improve the accountability of corporations to their ultimate owners, preferably by having corporations compete for investment, and institutional investors for funds, in part on the degree of accountability they offer to their beneficial owners.

The Institute of Economic Affairs
2 Lord North Street, Westminster, London SW1P 3LB
Telephone: 0171 799 3745 Facsimile: 0171 799 2137
E-mail: iea@iea.org.uk Internet: http://www.iea.org.uk

£12.00

ISBN 0-255 36416-4

Regulating European Labour Markets:

More costs than benefits?

John T. Addison and W. Stanley Siebert

1. The present British government has signed on to the social chapter, the provisions of which are now an integral part of the European Union treaties .
2. European Union social policy can be traced back at least to 1974 even though the treaty basis for social legislation is very narrow.
3. The extension of majority voting under the 1986 Single European Act mad it easier to pass social legislation. After the 'social charter' was proclaimed in 1989, legislative proposals 'came thick and fast', some making 'creative use' of health and safety criteria.
4. The 1997 Treaty of Amsterdam not only contains the provisions of the earlier Agreement on Social Policy but includes an employment chapter which '...opens up scope for considerable Commission activism in the future' and is a '...central plank of social policy'.
5. Market failure arguments may provide a basis for political intervention in the labour market but they are not clearcut. Furthermore, it is difficult to specify mandates which will deal adequately with market failures and government corrective action will itself be subject to failure.
6. Britain and other countries with less regulated labour markets have been better at creating employment opportunities than the more regulated major EU states.
7. Empirical studies generally show that the net effect of employment protection and similar rules is '...lower employment, greater and longer unemployment for some and, implicitly, a decline in the speed with which labour relocates from declining to growing sectors of the economy.'
8. Not all employment regulations will have the same effect. But the 'upwarc harmonisation sought by the Commission' has potentially serious costs in terms of 'disemployment and reduced employment growth'.
9. The Commission has failed to meet its obligation to evaluate the possible effects of its social proposals on the labour market. Its efforts have been amateurish and have taken place in an 'analytical vacuum'.
10. Its proposals should in future be subject to independent efficiency audit, not to prevent the development of social policy but to provide informatio on the employment and other consequences of new mandates.

The Institute of Economic Affairs
2 Lord North Street, Westminster, London SW1P 3LB
Telephone: 0171 799 3745 Facsimile: 0171 799 2137
E-mail: hwu@iea.org.uk Internet: http://www.iea.org.uk

£8.00

ISBN 0-255 3642